Family Child Care

Contracts and Policies

Becoming a Family Child Care Professional

Family child care is a special profession for those who love young children. As a professional family child care provider, you must balance the skills required to care for children with those required to operate your business. Here are some tips to help you do this:

- Learn the child care regulations for your area, and follow them.
- Join your local family child care association.
- Sign up with your local child care resource and referral agency.
- Join the Child and Adult Care Food Program (CACFP).
- Find good professional advisors (such as a tax preparer, insurance agent, lawyer).
- Actively participate in training to acquire and improve your professional skills.

Additional Resources

Redleaf Press and Redleaf National Institute are two leading national organizations that share the goal of helping your family child care business succeed. Redleaf National Institute (www.redleafinstitute.org; 651-641-6675) can answer your business questions; its Web site is filled with free handouts, articles, and newsletters. Redleaf Press (www.redleafpress.org; 800-423-8309) publishes resources for family child care. Redleaf offers five online business classes for college credit and the following publications to support your business. For more information, see www.redleafpress.org.

- Starting a family child care business:
  Getting Started in the Business of Family Child Care (free from www.redleafinstitute.org)
  From Babysitter to Business Owner by Patricia Dischler

- Promoting your business:
  Family Child Care Marketing Guide: How to Build Enrollment and Promote Your Business as a Child Care Professional

- Creating contracts and policies:
  Sharing in the Caring: Family Child Care Parent-Provider Agreement Packet

- Keeping accurate records and filing your taxes:
  Family Child Care Record-Keeping Guide
  Calendar-Keeper and *C-K Kids: The Online Calendar-Keeper*™, by Redleaf Press
  Family Child Care Tax Workbook and Organizer

- Reducing business risks:
  Family Child Care Legal and Insurance Guide: How to Reduce the Risks of Running Your Business

- Building support groups:
  Creating Connections: How to Lead Family Child Care Support Groups by Joan Laurion and Cherie Schmiedicke

- Managing your money and planning for retirement:
  Download articles from www.redleafinstitute.org.

(All publications are by Tom Copeland unless otherwise indicated.)

Family Child Care

Contracts and Policies

How to Be Businesslike in a Caring Profession

Third Edition

Tom Copeland, JD

featuring a CD-ROM with customizable worksheets
by Deloris Friske and Beth Mork, with Tom Copeland

Redleaf Press
www.redleafpress.org

Published by Redleaf Press
a division of Resources for Child Caring
10 Yorkton Court
St. Paul, MN 55117
Visit us online at www.redleafpress.org.

Redleaf Press books are available at a special discount when purchased in bulk for special premiums and sales promotions. For details, contact the sales manager at 800-423-8309.

Library of Congress Cataloging-in-Publication Data

Copeland, Tom.
  Family child care contracts and policies : how to be businesslike in a caring profession / Tom Copeland with Deloris Friske and Beth Mork.— 3rd ed.
      p. cm.
  Includes bibliographical references.
  ISBN-13: 978-1-929610-79-2
  ISBN-10: 1-929610-79-3
  1. Family day care—United States. 2. Family day care—Law and legislation—United States. 3. Contracts—United States. I. Friske, Deloris. II. Mork, Beth. III. Title.
  HQ778.63.C65 2006
  362.7'120687—dc22

                              2006001090

Printed in the United States of America.
13 12 11 10 09 08 07 06   1 2 3 4 5 6

Disclaimer
This book discusses a variety of legal issues, including the role of contracts and policies between family child care providers and their clients. Redleaf Press and the author are not engaged in rendering legal, accounting, or other professional services and are not responsible for the outcomes of how this information is interpreted or applied. If legal or expert assistance is required, the reader should consult the services of a qualified professional. All names used in this book are fictitious.

Contents

Acknowledgments

I would like to acknowledge a number of people who helped with previous editions of this book: Margareta Vranicar; Eileen Nelson; Debbie Hewitt; Anne Thompson; Diane M. Phillippi, LSW, family day care licensor, Ramsey County; Rose Cerato, field station manager and Lucy Tschogl, Las Vegas coordinator, America West Airlines Child Care Department; Abbey Cohen, Child Care Law Center; Madeleine Baker, Lincoln National Corporation; Pat Ward, Family Day Care Project, National Council of Jewish Women; Joe Perreault, Save the Children, Atlanta; Diane Adams, Child Care Coordinating Council, Madison, Wisconsin; and family child care providers Debra Goodlaxson, Lynne Coates, Darlene Tonga, and Stephen C. and Deborah A. Dietz.

I would also like to acknowledge the major contribution made by Phyllis Karasov, Esq., of Moore, Costello and Hart, St. Paul, Minnesota.

For this edition of the book I would like to thank Jennifer Allman, Sharon Anderson, Judy Boyd, Cindy Clark, Lori Dalto, Lucila Figuereo, Pat Gentz, Wendy Hintz, Donna S. Kirby, Mary Kowalski, Kathy Lee, Deb McCarthy, Kelly Mathews, Christen Partsafs, Jan Porter, Victoria Rossiter, and Natalie Short. A special thanks to Deloris Friske and Beth Mork.

I appreciate the many hardworking family child care providers whom I have met and talked with over the years. Their experiences have helped shape this book.

This book also received major assistance from Rose Brandt for editing and layout, Laurie Buss and Jeni Henrickson for project management, Ryan Scheife for production assistance, and Sid Farrar for coordination and management.

We Would Like Your Feedback

We would appreciate hearing your feedback about this book. Please contact us with any questions or suggestions for topics to add in future additions of this book. You can reach us at rni@redleafinstitute.org or 651-641-6675. We will post any changes or corrections to the information in this book on our Web site, www.redleafinstitute.org.

PART I

Establishing
Businesslike Relationships

CHAPTER ONE

Being Businesslike in a Caring Profession

Chapter Summary
This chapter introduces the importance of businesslike relationships in
family child care and the role that written contracts and policies play in
those relationships. It explains the tools included in this book and on the
accompanying CD to help you create your own customized contract and
policies.

Anyone can love a child, but it requires more than love to properly take care of one—and
it takes special skills and commitment to care for a group of children of different ages on a
day-to-day basis over a long period of time. This is the job of today's family child care
provider. It is a unique job that isn't comparable to any other profession.

As a family child care provider, you are a self-employed businessperson who has many
responsibilities—caring for children, dealing with clients, and managing a business—all
while continuing to care for your own family. Along with the rewards of running your own
business, there are also risks involved, such as injury to children, damage to property, or
becoming the target of a lawsuit. As every family child care provider knows, this job is far
from simple.

Learning to Balance Caring and Business

To be successful in your business, you will need to establish a professional, businesslike
relationship with the parents of the children in your care. This means that you will need to
take yourself and your work seriously and treat the parents of the children in your care as
business clients, even if they are also friends or relatives. You will be most successful if you
are able to distinguish and find a balance between the caring attention required for child care
and the businesslike focus required for managing your business.

The purpose of this book is to help you find that balance by explaining how to use written
contracts and policies to communicate more clearly and manage your business more smoothly. However, you don't have to follow every one of the suggestions that I make in this book.
If the arrangements that you currently have with your clients are working well for you, that's

great. I'm not suggesting that you change anything that doesn't need fixing. I simply recommend that you take from this book the ideas that make sense to you.

On the other hand, over the years I've found that when a provider calls me for advice about a conflict she's having with a client, she often says, "I've been in business for years, and I've never had this kind of problem before!" Since she didn't anticipate the kind of problem that arose, it took her by surprise and she wasn't prepared to deal with it.

Throughout this book I'll provide examples of the kinds of problems and conflicts that can arise between family child care providers and their clients. If you've been in business for a while and haven't experienced these kinds of problems, the examples may give you food for thought—and I hope that they will help you prepare for, or even prevent, potential problems that might otherwise take you by surprise.

● ●

Who Is This Book For?

For the purposes of this book, a "family child care provider" is anyone who works out of her home (or another home) caring for one or more children on behalf of the parents. She may only care for the children of relatives or close friends. She may be licensed, regulated, or certified, or she may be exempt from those rules. The information in this book applies to all family child care providers, regardless of their legal status.

Also, each state has different family child care regulations and legal terms; I will use the term "licensing" to refer to any state and local rules that regulate your business. By "licensed provider" I mean someone who meets her state and local regulations, and by "licensor" I mean the person (or agency) who enforces compliance with those rules.

● ●

Don't Treat Your Clients Like Friends

Some family child care providers find it very difficult to talk about money, rules, or expectations with their clients. One factor that can greatly complicate this is growing so close to the children in your care that you become emotionally involved in their parents' personal lives. This is a mistake. No matter how close you get to your clients, you still have to meet your responsibilities as a business owner—and your clients don't share that priority.

Treating your clients as friends blurs your priorities and makes it more difficult to manage your business wisely. Do you advertise your business by asking "Need a friend?" Does your contract say "If you sign this, I'll be your friend?" Obviously not. By treating your clients as friends, you send the message that you expect them to treat you as a friend, rather than as a businessperson; this isn't what the client is paying you for and makes it difficult to maintain businesslike expectations.

● ●

Parent or Client?

Most family child care providers refer to their clients as "parents"; however, this term refers to the parent-child relationship, not the parent-provider relationship. In this book, I'll use the term "client" when referring to the parent-provider relationship. A businessperson who provides a service does so on behalf of a *client*, and I encourage you to use this terminology. While this may seem too formal at first, it may help you to think more clearly about your business relationships and therefore be more successful in offering high-quality child care.

● ●

If you have ever felt disappointed that a client didn't return your overtures of friendship, bear in mind that the problem wasn't with the client. Your clients are looking for good child care, not a good friend. This doesn't mean that you can't have close relationships with your clients. You can go shopping together and do many of the things that friends do; however, you need to keep enough emotional distance that you don't abdicate your primary role as a business owner and caregiver.

On the other hand, you don't need to "go it alone," either. If you decide to make an effort to adopt a more professional attitude toward your business, ask your spouse and children for moral support. Explain the satisfaction you will feel at being a more successful business owner and child care provider, and how adopting more businesslike practices will improve your relationships with your clients, build your family's financial security, and enhance your peace of mind.

Do Your Clients Respect Your Business?

Do you find that some of your clients don't seem to treat family child care as a business? If so, there may be several possible reasons why. The client may have no idea what you do all day, how much his children are learning, how you manage your time, or how many hours you really work.

The child care clients of today are the last generation that didn't have family child care experience as children, and this kind of business is unfamiliar to them. This means that you have a big job to do in explaining it to them. A potential client who enters a child care center can look around and see that it is like a school for small children; but family child care takes place in a private home that doesn't look like a school or business.

And yet, the single biggest reason why many clients don't treat family child care as a business is that their family child care provider doesn't act as if she is running one. Establishing a healthy business relationship by clearly communicating your rules and expectations is necessary for reducing and resolving conflicts and bringing you the respect you deserve—and a written contract and policies are the most effective way to do that.

You Set the Rules for Your Business

As a family child care provider, you are a self-employed businessperson. One of the biggest benefits of this line of work is that you are your own boss and no one's employee. This means that you set your rules and policies, not your clients. You can operate a highly- or loosely-structured program. You can serve hamburgers or vegetarian food. You can care only for infants or exclude them. You can have hundreds of rules that your clients must follow or only a few rules. The type of service that you offer is strictly up to you. This is how it works in any business; your clients don't set the rules for your business, just as you don't tell your bank how to run its operations.

The first step in establishing a businesslike relationship with your clients is deciding how you would like to run your business; once you know that, you can put your policies into written form so that your clients will know what to expect. For many family child care providers, this isn't an easy task. If you feel hesitant about deciding how to run your business, bear in mind that there's no one else to do it for you—there's no director, manager, or supervisor but you. Since it is your business, you are responsible for everything—you are the activity planner, cook, cleaner, rule maker and enforcer, bill collector, salesperson, and manager.

Although it may feel overwhelming to have to make all these business decisions in addition to caring for the children, it falls to you alone to establish and maintain a businesslike relationship with your clients. You are the only person who can set, communicate, and enforce the rules for your business. Your clients will never ask me to teach them a class called "how to pay your child care provider on time."

What Are Contracts and Policies?

Unlike other books and sample contracts that you may have seen before, this book makes a clear distinction between contracts and policies, and recommends that you do likewise. Why is this important? Although I will explain the answer more fully in chapter 3, basically the advantage of keeping these documents separate is that this gives you maximum flexibility to change your policies when needed as well as maximum legal protection if you ever need to enforce the terms of your contract in court.

Since I will be using the terms *contract* and *policies* throughout this book, it may be helpful at this point to explain just what I mean by them:

- A *contract* is a binding legal agreement between two people. If you agree to care for a child and the child's parent agrees to pay you for that care, you have made a verbal contract. If you put the contract in writing, it becomes a written contract. When you make a contract, both parties expect the other to live up to the terms of the agreement. If that promise is broken, either party is entitled to seek payment for damages. (In the case of a family child care contract, the parties can only seek damages for the failure of the client to pay or the failure of the provider to deliver child care as stipulated in the contract.)

- In a family child care business, your *policies* are the rules that state (preferably in writing) how you will care for the children, handle specific kinds of situations, and run your business. For example, family child care policies typically cover how the children will be disciplined, what activities will be offered to the children, when meals will be served, how children with special needs will be cared for, and how illnesses and other kinds of emergencies will be handled.

• •

Legal Disclaimer

You shouldn't consider the legal statements that I make in this book to be my official legal opinion or the last word on the subject. Every situation is different, and if you need legal advice, you should consult an attorney. If you have questions about the practices or legal requirements in your local area, you can ask other providers, your family child care provider organization, your Food Program sponsor, your licensor, or the child care resource and referral agencies in your area.

• •

Tools for Writing Your Agreements

As an independent business owner, you are entitled to set up your contract and policies however you wish. The only constraint is that you cannot violate local, state, or federal law (see pages 66 and 75). Other than that, you are free to run your business as you wish. Since every family child care business is different, you'll need to decide for yourself what to put in your contract and policies; there isn't one set of terms that will work for everyone.

This book and the CD that comes with it include several tools to help you write your client agreements. In this book, Part II and Part III provide a detailed explanation of the terms and issues that you may want to cover in your contract and policies, including specific language that you can use. The appendixes of this book provide four samples that you can use as a model—three filled-in sample contracts and a sample policy handbook:

- The first sample contract uses only a few simple terms and is offered as a guide for those who prefer to use a basic and simple agreement.
- The second sample contract has more information and is written on an agreement form that you can order from Redleaf Press.
- The third sample contract is an example of a customized contract that you can create using the contract worksheets on the CD that comes with this book.
- The sample policy handbook in Appendix B is an example of a customized set of policies that you can create using the policy worksheets on the CD.

The three sample contracts in Appendix A are explained in more detail in chapter 3 (see page 27).

The CD That Comes with This Book

To make it easier to create your client agreements, this book comes with a CD that contains editable text for the contract terms and policy options discussed in this book. You can save the files on the CD to your computer and then select the specific language that you want to use. The worksheets on this CD are based on a workbook created by Deloris Friske and Beth Mork, who are family child care providers with many years of experience.

To use the worksheets on the CD to create your contract and policies, first save the worksheet files on the CD to your computer. Open each file, and remove all the options that you don't want to use. Edit the remaining terms and add any other information needed for your business, then format the documents as you wish. You can also customize a copy of the forms for each client. Finally, print out the documents for your clients to sign. (For more detailed instructions, see "How to Use This CD" on the CD.)

• •

If You Are an Illegal or Unregulated Provider

You can still use written contracts for all the purposes described in this book even if you are an illegal or unregulated provider. However, your contract probably won't be enforceable in court unless you disclosed to the client that you were illegal or unlicensed at the time she signed the contract. If you misled the client about your status, a judge is likely to rule against you. If you informed the client of it, then it probably won't hurt you in court. The bottom line is that written contracts and policies offer the same benefits to illegal and exempt providers who disclose their status to their clients as they do to licensed providers.

• •

Contracts Are the Basis of Business Relationships

In working with a business client, contracts and policies are used to establish the rules and expectations of the relationship; a businesslike relationship means that both parties follow those rules in good faith and treat each other with respect. On your part, this will require you to keep a certain emotional distance from your clients, which can be hard to do when you're so close to their children. However, that distance is necessary in order to provide the best care for the children and to ensure that you are fairly compensated for your work.

Being businesslike doesn't mean that you have to be rude or unsympathetic in order to deal successfully with your clients. There is no conflict between being a warm, caring person and presenting yourself in an organized, businesslike manner. When negotiating or enforcing a contract with a client, you can be tough without being cold-hearted. Being businesslike simply means sticking to your own rules and setting healthy limits. It is always appropriate to use assertive (rather than aggressive) behavior to state your policies and enforce your agreements. Although you can't please everyone, most of your clients will come to trust you because you are showing that you have given careful thought to the business of caring for their children.

Although the primary purpose of this book is to explain how to create and enforce written contracts and policies to support your business, it's important to bear in mind that these documents aren't substitutes for good communication. In the next chapter I'll explain that these agreements are actually just one kind of communication tool that you can use to set businesslike expectations with your clients. That chapter will provide the foundation for Parts II and III, in which I will discuss how to write the terms in your contract and policies.

CHAPTER TWO

Practicing Good Communication

Chapter Summary
This chapter describes the communication practices that can help you maintain good relationships with your clients. It includes tips that can help you set businesslike expectations and make it easier to talk about uncomfortable issues.

Some family child care providers can spend many happy hours talking with children and yet find themselves tongue-tied when it's time to communicate with their clients, especially about a business problem. This can lead to conflicts, since regular and effective communication is one of the most important ingredients in maintaining a good relationship with your clients.

One sign that you and your clients aren't communicating well is that you have chronic complaints about them, such as "They take advantage of me"; "They're inconsiderate and difficult to deal with"; or "They don't respect my business." However, when communication is poor, your clients are also likely to have legitimate complaints about you. When these differences aren't addressed, they can escalate and lead to serious consequences; in fact, they are one of the primary reasons that providers leave the child care field.

However, most client conflicts can be prevented or resolved before they become unmanageable by following businesslike communication practices. This includes establishing reasonable policies and finding effective ways to communicate them. By enforcing your rules and giving notice to clients who won't follow them, you send the message that you are able to set clear limits and control your business.

Of course, even the best communication can't guarantee that your business relationships will be free of problems and conflicts. It simply means that you will expect your clients to respect your policies, and they will have the right to complain if they aren't happy. However, when problems arise, a history of regular, honest communication will help resolve them more quickly or at least minimize the consequences to your business.

If a client's behavior is particularly difficult and she isn't willing to change it, good communication practices can help you enforce your contract or terminate the business relationship (see chapters 11 and 12). There are five steps that I recommend you follow to establish good communication with your clients:

1. Keep careful records.
2. Make a habit of communicating regularly.
3. Use tools to improve communication.
4. Record problems as they arise.
5. Use a written contract and policies.

Although some of these steps may appear to be more important than others, all five are necessary for communicating in an effective and businesslike way. The rest of this chapter will explain the importance of each step and provide suggestions for implementing it.

Keep Careful Records

To run a well-managed business, you need to keep good records. Certain records are mandatory; your state may require family child care providers to keep certain information, and you will need other information (such as your business income and expenses) in order to prepare your tax returns. In general, you will need to keep the following forms and information on file for your business:

- Your child care license
- The attendance records of the children in your program
- Your monthly claim forms for the Child and Adult Care Food Program
- Your business income and expenses
- Your tax returns
- Your business liability insurance policy
- Your employee records, if any
- Any other legal documents for your business (such as incorporation papers or the registration of your business name)

In addition to the above required records, you should also keep the following records for each child in your care:

- The contract and policies signed by the client (the child's parent or guardian)
- The child's enrollment forms
- Any medical records and medical authorization forms for the child
- The receipts for the client's payments
- The field trip permission forms signed by the client
- Your notes about the child's behavior and progress
- Your notes about any conflicts with that client
- Your general observations about the child or the family

Keeping these records in an organized way will make it easier to communicate with your clients, maintain businesslike relationships with them, and resolve any conflicts that may occur. In addition, by periodically reviewing these records you are likely to find ways to improve your business practices.

Communicate Regularly

Although written contracts and policies are powerful communication tools, they aren't meant to replace other, equally important, forms of communication with your clients. You should get into the habit of talking with your clients in a variety of ways and on a regular basis. It will be easier to discuss any problems that arise later in the relationship if regular communication habits are established from the beginning.

••

Talk to Both Parents

Whenever there are two adults who have custodial rights or are living with the child, it's important to establish regular communication with both of them, since they won't always see things the same way. This is especially important for divorced parents who share legal or physical custody. However, it also means that whenever there are two adults who are living together and caring for the child, you should meet with both of them—even if only one has legal custody or is the child's biological parent.

••

When you interview a new client (see chapter 9), you should explain the importance of regular communication and how you implement it in your business. For example, describe your policy of reviewing the child's day on a daily basis. Ask the client when, how, and how often he would like you to communicate with him. You may have to do some experimenting, but once you find out what works, establish a consistent pattern of communication for each client and stick with it.

Set a Time and Place for Business Conversations

Even if you're talking regularly with a client about her child, it can still be difficult to introduce a business topic, especially if you tend to be busy during drop-off and pickup times. To make sure that you have time to discuss business, set a regular time and method (usually a meeting or phone call) that is reserved for those issues. You might arrange to call the client after dinner on Wednesday, or the client might stay late to talk on Friday. If there isn't anything to discuss at the prearranged time, you can either cancel that session or just do a brief check-in.

It's also helpful to establish a specific place in your home for these discussions. The size of the space isn't important; it can be your living room or the corner by your desk. When you want to bring up a business matter, ask the client to come into this area. This will help signal that you are making a transition to talking about business.

● ●

If There's No Time to Talk, Write a Note

If a client is in too much of a hurry to talk when she picks up or drops off her child, you can use short notes to keep her informed on a daily basis. (Or you can call her in the evening, if that works better for her.) You can also suggest to your clients that they communicate with you via notes or e-mail, if that is easier for them. (If it gets to be too much to talk or write on a daily basis, try it on a weekly basis.) However, don't rely on written messages as a substitute for regular client meetings.

● ●

Hold Regular Client Meetings

In addition to communicating on a daily or weekly basis, it's a good idea to schedule a regular meeting with each client at least once every three months. If your schedules don't allow you to get together that often, aim for every six months, or at least have this conversation when it's time to renew your contract. If there are two parents (or more than one adult who has custody of or lives with the child), try to schedule these meetings with both of them, or meet with them separately.

At these meetings, sit down together and discuss how the child is doing and how your business arrangement is working. Review the goals that you and the clients have set for the child; show the clients some of the work that the child has done and describe her progress. Clients who regularly hear how their child is progressing in your program will be less likely to decide to change child care providers.

If the arrangement has been going well, your side of the business discussion can be very simple—tell the client what has been working well and ask for his perspective:

Things are running smoothly, Peter. I appreciated your willingness to bring an extra set of clothes for our field trip last week, and I thank you for regularly picking up Anna on time, even though I know you have a tight schedule. How has our arrangement been working for you?

If there have been problems in the arrangement, bring them up in a positive, constructive way and ask the client for help solving them:

Most things are working well between us, Peter, but we do have one problem. You know that our contract calls for you to pay me each Monday morning, and last week I didn't get paid until Wednesday. This is a problem for me, even if you pay me on Monday evening, because I need the money to cover the bills that I have to pay that day. I can't be flexible about this part of our contract. What can we do to correct this?

If the client brings up a problem at your meeting, listen and ask questions to make sure that you understand what, if anything, he would like you to do differently. Acknowledge the client's feelings about the situation, but don't get bogged down in the details of the problem. Try to focus on specific actions that you might take to address his concern. (See page 16 for more on handling client feedback). A regularly scheduled meeting can give both of you the opportunity to discuss problems before too much time has passed. When a problem arises, it's always better to notify a client promptly rather than to wait and suddenly surprise him with a series of complaints. (If the problem involves a violation of your contract or policies, see chapters 10 and 11.)

Ask Clients to Evaluate Your Program

In addition to regular communication and meetings, another way to improve communication is to ask your clients to fill out an evaluation form for your program. It's best to request an evaluation once a year and whenever a client leaves your program—clients who are leaving may have especially useful ideas or comments. Your evaluation form can be simple; you might ask clients to rate your program on a five-point scale from "needs improvement" to "wonderful" and ask them to respond to the following questions:

* What do you like best about my program?
* What could I do to improve my program?
* Is there anything you could do to improve the care your child receives here?
* Would you recommend me to other parents? Why or why not?
* Do you have any other comments?

(These five questions are included on the Evaluation Form on the CD.) The feedback that you get on this form will show you where you are doing well and will suggest possible areas for improvement. Here are some examples of typical responses:

What do you like best about my program?

* I love the way you give Keisha a warm welcome and a big hug each morning.
* Henry is always talking about the fun activities he does in day care, especially playing outside in your yard.

What could I do to improve my program?

* Nothing much. Sometimes I wish Mike wasn't so dirty when I come to pick him up.
* I wish your policy was more flexible about caring for Jolie after 6 PM. Sometimes it's a real problem leaving work to get there on time.

Is there anything you could do to improve the care your child receives here?

* I will try to remember to bring enough diapers at the beginning of the week so you don't run out.
* If it would help, I can bring the toys that Jimmy's outgrown for the other children to play with.

Would you recommend me to other parents? Why or why not?

- Yes, I am very satisfied with the care that Brent receives.
- No, because the house is too dirty and cluttered.

Do you have any other comments?

- There don't seem to be enough books and toys for my six-year-old.
- I particularly like the singing games that you share with my children. Thank you!

Use the Feedback to Head Off Problems

When you receive an evaluation form from a client, promptly arrange a phone or in-person meeting to review the issues and comments that she has raised—whether favorable or unfavorable—in a businesslike way. If her comments are favorable, you may want to ask her if you can use the evaluation as a reference for prospective clients.

If her comments aren't favorable, how should you deal with them? Before you respond, bear in mind that the complaint may or may not be valid, and that you will never be able to please everyone. Thank the client for her feedback, and try to consider her criticism objectively.

If the complaint is vague—"I don't like my child's daily schedule"—ask her to clarify it—"What would you like her to be doing differently?" If only one client has mentioned that particular complaint, you may be able to get more perspective on it by asking your other clients if they have experienced the same problem. (You might also ask your licensor; she is likely to have some insight into how your program compares with other family child care programs.)

If you believe that a complaint is valid—"Your house is too dirty and cluttered"—tell the client the steps you are taking to correct it—"I'm going to spend more time cleaning before the children arrive in the morning." If you believe that a complaint isn't valid—"I wish you were more flexible about caring for Jolie after 6 PM"—make it clear to the client that you have no plans to change it—"I'm sorry that you're unhappy about that, but I'm not willing to care for children after 6 PM, as spelled out in our contract."

Asking your clients to fill out the evaluation form is simply the first step. By promptly addressing any problems or issues that they raise, you can proactively correct minor problems before they fester and become major problems that could threaten your business.

Use Tools to Improve Communication

Although direct communication is best, some issues (such as payment problems) can be very difficult to raise directly with clients. It can also be difficult to establish a habit of businesslike expectations, especially if you haven't emphasized this before. One way to handle these kinds of problems is to use tools and props to clearly convey the businesslike nature of the transaction. This section will describe several examples of communication tools and how to use them.

Use Business Forms to Request Payments

What's the most difficult thing to say to a client? For many family child care providers, the answer would be, "You owe me money." Money can be a difficult topic to bring up in conversation. For example, let's say that it's payment day; Sandy is getting ready to leave with her child, and you aren't sure if she'll remember to pay you. If you say in a friendly way, "You owe me money!" she may take this as a casual remark, rather than a businesslike request for payment—and she might respond, "Oh, you don't really need the money now, do you?" The conversation is now about whether you really need the money, which isn't the issue.

A better way to handle this situation would be to use a business form such as a bill or receipt. Prepare the form before Sandy gets there, and have it ready to hand to her. When she arrives, give her the bill, or say, "You need to get your receipt before you leave today." Of course, before she can get her receipt, she must pay you. This is a businesslike way to bring up the subject and remind a client that it is payment day. You aren't asking her for the money; you are completing a scheduled business transaction.

Giving a client a bill or a receipt is an effective way of communicating that the client owes you money and is easier than asking directly for payment. Here are more ideas for handling payments in a professional manner:

Use Pay Boxes

On the day that payments are due, place a small box (like a shoe box) with a slit in the top in a prominent location where your clients will be sure to see it. Put a sign on the box that says "Insert payments here." This will remind your clients to deposit their money in the box and you won't have to say anything.

Treat Payments in a Businesslike Way

When you take a payment from a client, don't just put it in your pocket or lay it on the counter. Immediately write the client a receipt, and then put the payment in a place that is reserved for client payments—such as a desk drawer, cash box, folder, or manila envelope. By following the same routine every time you receive a payment, you show your clients that you are treating their transactions seriously and handling your income in a businesslike manner.

Put Your Rules in Writing

When you explain your rules and expectations to clients, do you find that they often try to argue with you, or that they challenge you at every turn? If so, part of the reason may be how you use your voice. Some providers speak clearly and decisively and don't have as many problems setting expectations for their business. Other providers have a soft or hesitant speaking voice that causes clients to think that they would be easy to overrule or don't really mean what they are saying.

Instead of trying to control your voice patterns (which can be difficult), I recommend that you make a habit of communicating your rules and expectations to your clients in written form to ensure a businesslike tone. A written statement not only conveys more authority than a verbal statement, it can also be used as a reminder later if the client forgets to follow it. Another benefit of written communication is that it can help you be more consistent and provide the same information to all your clients, especially if there are several families in your care. For example, one provider I know e-mails her bills to all her clients. She says this is easier than asking for payments and late fees face-to-face—she can be warm in person and businesslike in writing.

When you have a new rule to announce, write out an announcement and put it in a letter (if you will mail it) or a flyer (if your clients will pick it up). If you need to remind a client about the terms of your contract or policies, copy the original document, underline the relevant passages, and ask the client to read them. If the client says, "I'm busy; what does it say?" you can respond, "Once you read it over, I will be happy to answer any questions about it." Here are two more ideas for putting your business communications in writing:

Put up a Bulletin Board

Keep your clients informed by putting up a bulletin board in a spot where they will see it when picking up their children. On the board, post your business reminders and announcements and any upcoming menus, special events, activities, or field trips. Also consider posting other items of interest, such as information about family-friendly weekend activities in your area.

Write a Monthly Newsletter

Instead of a bulletin board, you could write a short (one- or two-page) monthly newsletter to keep your clients informed. You might announce your menus for the coming month, a policy reminder, a new rule, an upcoming special event, a rate increase, or a reminder to sign a trip permission form. You could also include previous-month highlights from your program, Q & A about your program, and client feedback (with permission from the client).

Record Problems as They Arise

Most of the problems that family child care providers are confronted with don't arise out of the blue—they usually start with small incidents that are never resolved. To keep this from happening, I suggest that you make a habit of briefly recording every noteworthy or unusual incident that involves a child or a client in your program. Although these notes are mostly designed to record problems, you can also note positive incidents or comments. File the notes by the client family involved (see page 12 for other records to keep in that file).

Let's look at an example to see how these notes can be useful. One afternoon Charlie and Denise are happily playing in the sandbox; then Charlie suddenly bites Denise, without any warning. After handling the situation, you make a note in your records:

May 12: Charlie bit Denise without any warning.

That evening you talk to Charlie's father, Ray. Neither of you can think of any reason for the incident. You decide to watch Charlie closely and keep detailed records of his behavior. After two weeks, you have recorded:

Notes on Charlie Baldwin—May

May 12: Charlie bit Denise without any warning.

May 14: Charlie bit Nancy at noon and again at 4 PM.

May 15: Charlie bit Denise during an argument about who would get to use a toy. Another biting at noon without any apparent reason.

May 19: Charlie bit Denise while we were deciding who gets to use the Big Wheel first.

May 21: Charlie bit Denise at 11:30 AM.

May 22: Charlie bit Nancy at 12:15 PM.

May 26: Charlie bit Denise at 4:30 PM.

On May 28, you have your regularly scheduled meeting with Ray, who says again that he can't think of any reason for Charlie's behavior. Reviewing your notes, you report that Charlie appears to bite Denise most often. Why? Maybe they aren't getting along? Also, Charlie often seems to bite around noon. Is he tired or hungry? Would an earlier lunch help him? Is he biting because he's not getting his way? How can you start narrowing down the possibilities? You and Ray eventually agree that Charlie and Denise should be kept apart for the next week, to see if that helps. If it doesn't, the next step will be to try moving his lunchtime up to 11:30. You make a note of these decisions in your records.

In this case, your records were helpful to both you and Ray in suggesting some options for dealing with Charlie's behavior. Without the notes, it would have been hard to tell who was bitten the most or when the biting occurred. If Charlie's problem continues and Ray decides to seek professional help for him, your notes will be very useful and may lead to faster treatment. By making short notes you have been able to promote communication with your client and enhance the quality of care for his child.

Use a Written Contract and Policies

Like regular meetings, invoices, and newsletters, your written contract and policies are tools that help you communicate clearly and set businesslike expectations for your clients. As you absorb the information about contracts and policies in the rest of this book, bear in mind that the primary purpose of these agreements is to facilitate communication. They enable you to avoid misunderstandings and confusion and to control the terms under which you do business. Although it's important to understand the legal implications of your contract, very few contract disputes ever wind up in court. So the most practical reason for using a contract and policies is to ensure that both parties understand what is expected of them.

Also bear in mind that your contract and policies are living documents and writing them will be an ongoing process. If you and your clients sign those agreements and then never look at them again, they won't be very useful communication tools. Your contracts and (especially) your policies should be updated as needed to reflect new circumstances.

● ●

Q & A: Getting Started with a Contract

Q: I've been a child care provider for a long time but I've never used a contract before. How can I begin using one?

A: You can start using a contract at any time. First, create your contract using the CD that comes with this book. Then schedule a meeting with each of your clients to discuss the agreement. Give your clients at least two weeks' advance notice that you will begin operating under a written agreement. If a client asks, "We've gotten along fine so far, why do we need a contract now—don't you trust me?" you can respond:

> *I'd like to use a contract so that we can more easily remember our verbal agreements and resolve any differences that might arise. I think it's a good idea to write down our expectations of each other and review them periodically to make sure that things are running smoothly.*

Insist on a deadline by which all your clients must sign the contract. If one of your clients refuses to sign it, notify her that she will need to find another child care arrangement by that deadline.

● ●

Putting Your Contract in Writing

Some providers are reluctant to establish firm rules for their business and put their client agreements in writing. They feel that it is easier to proceed informally and keep everything casual, at least as long as things are going well. There could be several reasons for taking this position. The provider might not be sure what to expect of her clients or herself; she might be eager to build her reputation; or she might be so eager to please her clients that she is willing to enroll their children at all costs.

Other providers are afraid that they will alienate or lose their clients if they try to create a more formal business relationship. Some of them even feel that a written agreement is at odds with their main purpose of caring for children.

However, I have found that most experienced child care providers are convinced that a written contract and policies are a necessary part of operating their business. In fact, many clients welcome a written agreement and consider it to be a sign that the provider is organized, responsible, and easy to communicate with. A provider who has a set of well-crafted written policies can actually use them as a selling point to attract clients.

A written contract serves many purposes:

- It makes both parties aware that they are entering into a serious, formal business agreement that they must honor.
- It reminds both parties of what they have promised to do.
- It helps to resolve conflicts by explaining the consequences of violating the contract.
- In the case of an unresolved conflict, it can be used by either the provider or the client to support a legal case.

A set of written policies also serves many purposes:

- It forces both parties to take steps to protect the child's health and safety by planning ahead for emergencies.
- It describes the program's procedures, thereby clarifying the expectations of both parties and reducing the client's anxiety about leaving her child with the provider.
- It helps the provider be organized and offer more consistent, reliable care.

What's Wrong with a Verbal Contract?

Although I strongly recommend that you use a written contract, a contract doesn't have to be in writing to be a legal agreement. However, it is very difficult to enforce a verbal contract in court, and a verbal contract can be terminated immediately by either party—which means that you may lose a paying customer without warning. Also, a verbal contract works well only as long as you and the client are in complete agreement about what it means, and that is nearly impossible. So it's difficult for a verbal contract to serve its primary purpose of improving communication, since you need to have nearly perfect communication for it to work in the first place.

For example, take the following scenario: One afternoon Juanita agrees to pay Sandy $100 a week to care for her child Monday through Friday from 7 AM to 5:30 PM. At this point, Sandy and Juanita have made a verbal contract. Although the agreement sounds clear enough, how would Sandy deal with the following situations:

- On Wednesday, Juanita's child is sick and stays home that day. Does Juanita need to pay Sandy the full $100 for that week?
- The next Tuesday, Juanita doesn't pick up her child until 7:30 PM—two hours later than usual. How much does Juanita owe Sandy for that week?
- The first week Juanita pays Sandy on Monday; the second week she pays on Wednesday; and the third week she pays on Friday. What can Sandy do to make sure she is paid on Monday each week?

It can be very difficult to enforce a verbal contract. Let's say that Juanita doesn't agree to pay for the days that her child is sick—but Sandy had expected to receive $100 a week, no matter how many days the child came. After arguing about it, they still don't agree. Sandy could take her case to a small-claims court and tell the judge that Juanita owes her for the sick days because that is what she understood when she agreed to care for Juanita's child.

At that point it will be up to the judge to decide what mutual understanding the two parties had when they made the verbal agreement. As the party bringing the lawsuit, Sandy has the burden of proof; she has to prove that there was mutual agreement in their verbal contract. Since this would be nearly impossible for her to do, the judge would probably rule against her.

Consider how different things would be if Sandy and Juanita had a written contract for their agreement. After talking it over, they might have agreed to something like this:

> *The usual weekly rate will be charged even if the child misses care for one or two days per week because she is sick. For more than two days of illness per week, the fee will be reduced by $10 for each day missed.*

Of course, Sandy and Juanita could have come up with another solution, such as waiving the child care fee for any sick days. The point is that if they had clarified this issue in writing, it is unlikely that they would ever have ended up in court. And if another problem had arisen—such as Juanita's child missing an entire week of care because of sickness—a written contact that explained how to handle one or two sick days would have made it easier for a judge to decide whether Juanita owes Sandy for that week.

How to Get Started

If you haven't used written agreements before, you probably have many questions at this point—you may be looking forward to actually writing your contract and policies, or you may be intimidated by the thought of putting all your expectations in writing. Although it may seem like a lot of work, this book and the accompanying CD can make the process of developing those documents relatively easy, and they can be as simple or as complex as you like. But first, be sure to read Part II of this book, which explains the language that you should put in your contract, and Part III, which discusses the policies that you may want to consider.

PART II

Writing Your Contract

CHAPTER THREE

What Should Be in Your Contract?

Chapter Summary
This chapter explains the difference between your contract and your policies, and introduces the key elements that you should include in your contract. It describes the three sample contracts provided in the back of this book and covers other issues about writing your contract, such as copyright.

There are important differences between the roles of contracts and policies, and therefore between the terms that you should include in your contract and those that you should include in your policies. Unfortunately, most family child care agreements tend to confuse these two categories, and this can create problems for both the provider and the client. Before you start writing your contract and policies, you should have a general understanding of these two kinds of documents and the differences between them.

The most significant difference is that contracts are legally enforceable, and policies aren't. However, this doesn't mean that you can put anything you want in your contract and a court will enforce it. It means that you should put in your contract the terms of your relationship that are enforceable by a court, which essentially means your agreements about time and money. Most of the terms of your policies aren't legally enforceable, since a judge will never tell you how to run your business or how to care for the children. She will only enforce the terms regarding the hours of service that you provide and how you will be paid for those hours. She won't enforce a statement that you will take the children on three field trips every week.

For this reason, you should put all stipulations about time and money, including a description of all your fees and charges, in your contract rather than in your policies. Your contract should state the hours that you will provide care and the amount that the client will pay you for that care, as well as any other possible charges, such as late fees. If you are available to provide the care during the stipulated time and your client refuses to pay the amount stated in the contract, you can sue her for breaking the contract (in legal terms, for "nonpayment of the fee"). If you refuse to provide care as described in the contract, she can sue you for breaking the contract (technically, for "failure to deliver the care").

On the other hand, if you have made it a policy that your clients are required to provide a change of clothing, you can't sue a client who fails to do so and ask for damages. If you have a policy that you will serve lunch every day, and you fail to do so, a client will have difficulty winning a judgment against you. If you and a client have an unresolvable conflict over a policy violation, your final recourse is simply to terminate the business relationship.

Another key reason to put your contract and policies in two separate documents is that when you combine them you limit your flexibility to make changes and respond to new circumstances. If your policies are separate from your contract, you can change them whenever you want and simply inform your clients of the change. But if those policies are described in your contract, you will have to rewrite your contract to include the new terms, and then convince all your clients to sign off on the new terms before you can put them into effect.

Although you will need to update your contract from time to time as your rates go up or if you want to adjust the terms (see chapter 10), a contract is intended to be a binding and long-lasting document. If you put the details of how your program operates (such as nap times, daily schedules, and how you'll respond to behavior problems) in your contract, over time those terms are likely to become increasingly fixed, limiting your ability to make changes. This isn't in the best interest of you, your clients, or the children in your care.

And finally, if you put your policies into your contract, you will run the risk of a client coming up with an argument such as, "You aren't feeding the children an afternoon snack every day as your contract states, so I don't have to pay you the full amount of our agreement." If you keep your contract and policies separate, it will be clear that your clients owe you the amount stated in the contract as long as you are open for business at the hours specified there.

The Key Elements of Your Contract

Unfortunately, there isn't one contract that will magically meet everyone's needs. Many family child care providers have based their contract on another provider's contract or one of the sample contracts that are circulating around the country. Your local licensor may have a sample contract or may even require you to use a contract that her office has prepared. Although a sample contract can be useful as long as it covers all the terms that you want to include, don't hesitate to change the language or to add or remove sections to fit your needs.

Your contract can be short or long. It doesn't have to be reviewed by a lawyer or contain fancy language. (If you're thinking of consulting an attorney, see the *Family Child Care Legal and Insurance Guide* for help.) Your contract doesn't have to be typed, although that does make it easier to read. However, there are five elements that you do need to include in every written contract:

1. The names of the parties to the contract
2. Hours of operation
3. Terms of payment
4. Termination procedure
5. The signatures of the parties to the contract

The next chapter includes a detailed discussion of the issues related to the names of the parties, your hours of operation, your termination procedures, and the signatures on your contract. The topic of terms of payment is far more complex than the other four elements, and I will devote an entire chapter to it (chapter 5).

The Sample Contracts in Appendix A

To give you a model for what your completed contract might look like, Appendix A includes three filled-in sample contracts. Although those samples vary in length and detail, they each contain all five of the key elements of a contract.

Sample Contract 1: Basic Contract

Sample Contract 1 is a simple, bare-bones agreement that just covers the basics. If you have not used a contract before, or if you're just starting your business, you may want to keep your client agreement as simple as possible to give yourself the flexibility to make adjustments as you go along. A short contract may also be sufficient if you care for just one child or aren't planning to be in business for long. Even this simple agreement can be an effective way to formalize your business relationship with your clients—although it's very brief, it still contains all five of the key elements. Also notice that it includes a statement that you may end the relationship without giving notice (see page 38) and a statement that the client must abide by your policies and that you may change them at any time (see pages 39–40).

Sample Contract 2: Child Care Agreement Form

Sample Contract 2 is handwritten on a two-page form you can order from Redleaf Press, the "Provider-Parent/Guardian Child Care Agreement." (This form is included in the *Sharing in the Caring* sample packet.) Although the form is still relatively short, it contains much more information than the first sample. However, it is still only an elaboration of the five key elements. Also, although this agreement covers more of the basic information, it still doesn't cover some other topics that you may want to add, such as your rate increases, damage to your property, extra services that you might provide, care before and after school, and so on.

Sample Contract 3: Fully Customized Contract

Sample Contract 3 is a fully customized contract like one you might create from the contract worksheets on the CD. The worksheets are organized by the five key elements; when you select the terms for your contract, be sure to cover all five of those areas, even if only briefly. The worksheets include specific wording for many options in each area of the contract, which allows you to make your contract as simple or as comprehensive as you wish.

To create your contract from the worksheets, save them to your computer, remove the options you don't want, edit the remaining options, and add any other information for your business. You can format the text as you wish—for example, by adding the logo for your business. The electronic format also makes it very easy to update your contract or to create a customized version of your contract for each of your clients.

Include a Trial Period in Your Contract

Signing a contract with a new client is a serious matter, and you want to make sure that the relationship will last. For this reason, I suggest that you start each new client with a short trial period that allows you to get to know each other with little risk.

A trial period is a limited period of time (usually one or two weeks) during which either party may end the relationship at any time. In other words, if the child care begins on Monday and the client is not satisfied for any reason, he could say on Tuesday, "I don't think this is working out" and immediately terminate the agreement. When this happens, you would charge him only for the days that you actually provided child care. You could also end the agreement yourself during the trial period.

Like your long-term contract, a trial-period agreement should be defined in writing and signed by both you and the client. To set up a trial period, you could write a separate document such as the following:

> *A trial period of child care will begin on Monday, March 10, 20xx. The client will pay $125 per week. During this time, either the client or the provider may cancel the contract immediately without written notice. If the contract is cancelled during this two-week trial period, the client will pay a prorated fee. Payment is due for each day unless the contract is cancelled before the day begins.*

Once you sign and date this agreement, you're ready to begin the trial period. To continue care after the trial period is over, the client would need to sign your regular contract. Another option is to have the client sign your regular contract before the trial period begins and include the following language in it:

> *Child care will begin on Monday, March 10, 20xx. The client will pay $125 per week. The first two weeks in the child care program will be an adjustment or trial period. During this time, either the client or the provider may cancel the contract immediately without written notice. If the contract is cancelled during this two-week trial period, the client will pay a prorated fee. Payment is due for each day unless the contract is cancelled before the day begins.*

• •

Can a Client Cancel Your Contract after Signing?

Some states have laws that allow consumers to cancel a contract within a few days after they sign it. These laws are primarily intended to protect a person who signs a contract for a car or other big-ticket item that is sold in a high-pressure situation. In most states these laws do not apply to your contract to provide child care. To find out if your state has any laws that apply to your contract, you can contact your state attorney general's office.

• •

Avoid Contradictions in Your Contract

As you write your contract, it's important to make sure that the terms don't contradict each other. For example, let's say that your contract requires your clients to give you a two-week notice before leaving and to pay for those two weeks even if their child isn't in your care. However, another clause states that clients don't have to pay you for the weeks that you take as vacation. This creates a loophole in your rules—what if one of your clients decides to give you her two-week notice (paid) on the day before you leave on a one-week vacation (unpaid). Can you require her to pay for both weeks? No; the problem is that one part of your contract says that she has to pay and another says that she doesn't have to pay. A contract that contradicts itself can't be enforced.

Here's another example of contradiction in a contract. Your contract requires clients to pay you for eight holidays a year, and it also allows them to take a two-week vacation without pay. So how would you handle a client who decides to take her vacation over the Fourth of July weekend?

To avoid these kinds of problems, address the issue of potential contradictions in the contract itself; for example, here are two clauses that do that:

- *The client must pay for the two-week notice period regardless of any other term in this contract.*

- *The client must pay for the paid holidays listed in this contract, regardless of any other term in this contract.*

State That Your Contract Will Be Enforced

Your contract may end up as a simple one-page document or several pages that include many of the terms described in the next two chapters. Regardless of how long it is, it's important to state in your contract that its terms will be enforced. Using a contract without actively enforcing its terms can lead to a lot of problems (see chapter 11).

For example, let's say that your contract requires your clients to pay a late fee, but you aren't assertive about asking for that fee every time a client is late. If you later try to collect a field trip fee, a client might object by saying, "You aren't enforcing your late fee rules, so I shouldn't have to pay your field trip fee. If you don't enforce all your rules, I don't have to follow any of them." To prevent this kind of argument, you can include the following language in your contract (see page 40):

A failure to enforce one or more terms of this contract does not waive the provider's right to enforce any other terms of this contract.

This will make it easier for you to enforce your rules selectively if you want to. However, the best approach is still to make an effort to consistently enforce all of the terms of your contract. If you can't do that, then consider eliminating the rules that you have difficulty enforcing from your contract. It's better to have no written rule about an issue than to have a written rule that you aren't enforcing.

• •

Don't Put a Liability Waiver in Your Contract

Some providers try to reduce the risk of a lawsuit by putting language in their contract that releases them from liability, such as:

Client agrees to hold provider harmless for any injuries suffered by the child during day care hours.

These liability waivers are invalid and won't hold up in court. Since your clients (and their children) can't give up their right to sue you, you shouldn't include this kind of statement in your contract. The best way to protect yourself from liability is to buy adequate business liability insurance (for more information, see the box on page 91 and the *Legal and Insurance Guide*).

• •

Subsidy Programs Have Their Own Rules

Many family child care providers care for children from families who receive government subsidies for their child care expenses. Although the subsidy may not pay you as much as you charge your other clients, I recommend that you participate in these programs since they are important for low-income families. However, when you participate, you and your subsidized clients must follow the rules of the subsidy program, which may be different from the rules in your contract for private payment clients.

You should make sure that you understand what your contract can and can't require a subsidized client to do. For example, the subsidy program may or may not allow you to charge the client for your holidays and vacations; it may or may not allow you to charge late pickup fees or a registration fee.

Before you sign a contract with a subsidized client, ask for written confirmation that the client is eligible to receive financial assistance and has filled out the proper paperwork. Know the deadlines that you and your client need to meet to ensure that you are paid in a timely manner. If you have any questions about the program, find someone in the local government agency who can answer them.

Before you provide care for a subsidized client, you should also check the rules of the subsidy program and decide if you will be able to abide by them. Some providers believe that they can't charge their private payment clients more than they receive from the subsidy program for their subsidized clients. This is often not true; in most (but not all) states you are allowed to charge your private clients more. Also, most of these programs (but not all of them) allow you to charge your subsidized clients an additional copayment if your private payment rates are higher than the subsidized rate. However, in some cases the state sets the amount of the copayment, and you can't charge more than that.

Your contract should state that the subsidized client is responsible for paying the full amount of your fee if the subsidy program doesn't pay you for any reason. You want to make sure that you can ask the client to pay that debt, if you have to.

Do You Need to Copyright Your Agreements?

Some family child care providers spend a lot of time developing their contract and policies and then share these documents with other providers. If you are concerned that someone might copy your materials, you should know something about copyright law. Anything that you write is given automatic copyright protection as soon as you write it; it isn't necessary to put "©" or "copyright" on your documents to get this protection. However, this can be a way to discourage others from copying your materials. So if you like, you can put the following notice at the bottom of the first page of your contract and policy handbook:

> © [year] *by* [your name]. *To reproduce this document you must receive written permission in advance from* [your name].

If someone else tries to copy your materials without your permission, you can stop her if you can prove that you were the original author; for example, by showing a copy of your contract or policies that was signed by one of your clients before the other person started using it.

If you would like more protection for your contract and policies, you can register your copyright with the federal government. This establishes that you are the author without having to prove it in court. For more information about how to register your copyright, visit the Library of Congress copyright office on the Web at www.copyright.gov. They have an excellent publication called *Copyright Basics*.

● ●

You Can't Copyright Any Material from This Book or CD

Bear in mind that you can't copyright any material that you copy from this book or CD, including the examples given in this book, the options provided on the contract and policy worksheets, or the language in the sample contracts and sample policy handbook shown in Appendix A and Appendix B.

● ●

CHAPTER FOUR

The Key Elements of Your Contract

Chapter Summary
This chapter explains the options and issues related to writing four of the elements of your contract—the names of the parties, your hours of operation, your termination procedure, and the signatures of the parties.

In this chapter I will discuss four of the elements of a contract in detail—the names of the parties, the hours of operation, the termination procedure, and the signatures of the parties. (The process of actually terminating a contract is covered in chapter 12; here I will simply explain what your contract should say about the termination process.) Since the topic of terms of payment is much more complex, I will cover it in detail in the next chapter; here I will just highlight the most important points. For the other four elements, this chapter will fully explain the issues and options that you should consider in selecting the terms of your contract.

Whether your contract is simple or complex, it should cover all of the five elements outlined in the previous chapter in some way. Before you write your contract, think about what you want it to say. Remember that you are free to choose your own terms, and that you need to feel comfortable with the contracts that you will be signing and operating your business under.

The Names of the Parties to the Contract
It's important that your contract clearly state the names of the parties to the contract and the children who are covered by the agreement. If you will be caring for more than one child in a family, be sure to list the names of all the children you will be caring for. Some providers prepare separate contracts for each child, but you don't have to do that. In fact, if you're giving the parents a discount because you're caring for more than one child, it's best to list all the children in the same agreement.

If the parents are married or living together, it's to your advantage to include both of them in the contract, because this means that you'll be able to collect payment from either one. In fact, whenever there are two adults who are living together and caring for the child, it will be helpful to get both of them to sign your contract, even if only one of them has legal custody. If only one parent has custody, ask for a copy of the custody order, because you will need to follow what the court has ordered (see pages 89–90). If the parents are a gay or lesbian couple, one or both of them will have legal custody of the child; ask if there are any custody orders and handle their signatures on your contract in the same way as any other client.

This section of your contract should list the name, address, e-mail address, phone numbers (including emergency contact numbers such as a cell phone or pager), and place of employment for each client who is signing your contract. (In addition to the obvious reasons for getting this information, you will need the client's current address and place of employment if you ever have to collect money after a court judgment—see chapter 13.)

Contracts with Single, Separated, and Divorced Parents

When a single parent asks you to care for her child, ask her about the status of the child's other parent—are they separated, divorced, or never married? If there is a court-ordered custody agreement, get a copy of it (see the *Legal and Insurance Guide* for information about how the legal aspects of shared custody agreements can affect your business).

Increasingly, divorced parents are being granted some type of joint or shared custody, which means that you're likely to be dealing with both parents. If the parents are sharing the responsibility for picking up and dropping off the child from your care, does this mean that they should both sign your contract?

Since a contract is about payment in exchange for services, I recommend that you only list the parent who pays you directly as a party to your contract. If both parents pay you directly, then include them both in the contract, and have them both sign it. They should both sign the same contract, since they are paying for the care of the same child (if they don't get along, you can meet with the parents separately to discuss and sign your contract and policies).

If the parents aren't living together and the mother is signing your contract, but you are aware that the father is paying her for part of the child care, make sure she understands that she is responsible for the entire payment, even if he fails to pay her.

• •

Terms for the Parties to the Agreement

The language in your contract and policies may refer to you and your client by name (as "Paul Parent" and "Sally Provider"), by using pronouns ("you" and "I"), or as the "client" and "provider." As long as it is clear who you are referring to, there is no legal difference between these approaches. In this book and in the worksheets on the CD, I will usually use the terms "client" and "provider" in the contract language, and the terms "you" and "I" in the policy options. However, you are free to change these terms if you wish, as shown in the three sample contracts in Appendix A.

• •

Hours of Operation

The section of your contract that covers your hours of operation should describe the time period covered by the contract, including the starting date of the contract and the hours that you will provide child care each day. It is important to clearly state what periods of time the client is paying you for and to describe your payment terms for any exceptions or absences that occur during those times.

Starting and Ending Dates

You should include the starting date of the child care in every contract. For example:

The first day of care will be Monday, October 3, 20xx.

If you don't include the starting date, there may be some confusion about when the terms of the contract will go into effect. However, you shouldn't include an ending date in a contract—there's no good reason to do so, and it can only cause problems for you.

For example, let's say that you use an annual contract that ends on December 31 each year. On December 1 you give all your clients a copy of your new contract to sign, but one of them doesn't get around to signing it, and you forget about it until January. If you have listed December 31 as the ending date of your previous contract, then you no longer have a valid written contract with that client, which means that after that date she will be able to leave without giving you any notice.

Hours of Child Care

Your contract should specify the starting and ending times of your care for each child. For example:

The hours of care will be from 6:30 AM to 5:30 PM, Monday through Friday.

If you don't do that, the client may assume that she can leave the child in your program as long as you're open for business. If she notices that you're caring for other children after that time, she may assume that she can pick up her child later, too. However, you may have many reasons for controlling when your clients come and go—you may need to plan meals, stay within the legal limits of your enrollment, or just make sure that you get some break time.

You also don't want a client to assume that if her child is enrolled in your program for 11 hours a day, she can bring the child for any 11-hour period during the day. In other words, you don't want her to think that it's okay to show up thirty minutes late in the morning and then pick up the child thirty minutes late in the afternoon. Another way to make sure this is clear is to include a statement in your contract such as "Late drop-offs do not allow for late pickups."

Handling Drop-ins and Exceptions

Once you set your hours, you need to honor them. This means that if a regular client notifies you that her child will miss a day and you want to fill that temporary vacant spot with a drop-in child, you will first need to get a written, signed release for that day from your regular client. Otherwise, if the regular client changes her mind and brings her child after all, you will need to send the drop-in child home (unless you are able to take both children). It doesn't matter whether your contract says that clients do or don't have to pay when their child isn't in your care. (Since this written release is actually a modification to your contract, you should file it with the client's contract.)

Here's an example: Your contract states that you will provide care for Sasha from 6 AM to 6 PM, Monday through Friday. On Monday night, Sasha's mother, Jill, calls you and says that she will be keeping Sasha home on Friday because she's taking the day off work—so you arrange to take a drop-in child on Friday to fill the spot. However, at 9 AM Friday, Jill calls to say that she's been called into work, and needs care for Sasha after all. Can you refuse to provide care in this case? No, since you have contracted to provide care during that time.

The answer would be different if you had asked Jill to drop off a signed note on Tuesday morning stating that she would not be bringing Sasha to care on Friday. If you had such a note from Jill, you could refuse to provide care for Sasha on Friday. But without a written modification to your contract, a regular client will always have the right to child care at the times stipulated in your agreement.

Setting Different Hours for Different Clients

Your hours of operation don't have to be the same for every child in your care; in fact, there may be good reasons to arrange different hours with different clients. If your workday normally begins at 7 AM, you can still arrange to begin care for one client at 6 AM because you only want to have one child that early in the morning or to temporarily give a client a helping hand in special circumstances.

In the same way, if your workday normally ends at 6 PM, you can still decide to stay open until 11 PM to help a client who is having a family emergency. This doesn't mean that you have to extend your workday for any other child in your program.

Since it's your business, it's up to you to determine your hours of operation (and every other term in your contract). One provider told me that she sets her hours for each client so that she only provides care when the parents can't be with their children. She won't care for a child if one of the parents is home—to calculate a client's pickup time, she finds out when he gets off work and adds the time he will need to get to her home. Her rationale is that it's important for parents to spend as much time with their children as possible. However, most providers don't have such a strong position and will provide child care for a set number of contracted hours, regardless of what the parents are doing.

Terms of Payment

Your contract should contain a complete statement of your terms of payment and all the issues related to the financial transactions between you and your client. I will cover this topic in detail in the next chapter. However, the most important recommendations for the terms of payment in your contract can be boiled down to two clauses that I recommend you put in every child care contract that you sign (for more information, see pages 46–49):

- *The client will pay for child care one week in advance.*

- *The client will pay for the last two weeks of child care upon signing this contract.*

In my experience, these are the two most important suggestions in this entire book. If you start using a contract just to enforce these two requirements, you will be likely to save yourself a lot of trouble someday.

Termination Procedure

A contract needs to include a process for ending the agreement, and the termination procedure section of your contract should explain that process and the consequences if it isn't followed. Also, the notice requirements for you and your client should be different.

When a Client Wants to End the Contract

When a client wants to terminate your contract, your contract should require her to give you advance written notice before she leaves. The purpose of this requirement is to give you time to make other arrangements before the contract ends. Without it, you could lose income while you are looking for another client.

A two-week notice requirement is most common across the country. Some providers require a longer notice, but most don't require more than a month. If you stipulate a longer notice, say six months or a year, and a client leaves before that time is up, the courts probably won't enforce it. I don't recommend that you ask clients to sign a one-year contract and expect them to pay for that year if they leave before the time is up.

You should require the client to give you the notice in writing. A client will often tell you that she's leaving and not honor this requirement. If she pays you for the full notice period (or if you have a deposit for that time), then this isn't a problem. However, a verbal notice could lead to a misunderstanding about exactly when she gave notice, or even if she gave notice at all. For example, let's say that you have the following conversation with a client:

Client: "I'm not happy about how you're treating my child. I don't feel as if you want my child in your program anymore."

You: "Well, you need to do what you need to do."

You might understand this conversation to mean that the client has given you notice to end the contract. The client might think that you are telling her not to come back and are thus terminating the contract. To avoid miscommunication, you should always take the responsibility to clarify whether the client is ending the contract. So a better response to this client would be, "Does this mean that you want to end our agreement?"

Your contract should clearly state that the client is required to pay you for the notice period, even if she leaves before it is over. I have seen contracts that include language such as:

- *The client must give a two-week written notice before leaving.*

- *The client must give a courtesy two-week notice before ending the contract.*

The problem with these examples is that a court can't enforce this language since the contract doesn't say what will happen if the client doesn't give the notice. Your contract will be unenforceable if it doesn't specify a consequence for failing to give the notice (see page 120). For this reason, the best language to put in your contract for ending the agreement is the following:

> *The client must give a two-week written notice to end this contract. Payment is due for the notice period whether or not the child is brought to the provider for care during that time.*

When You Want to End the Contract

It's common to require clients to give you a two-week notice before they can end a contract; however, I don't recommend that you extend this requirement to yourself—you should retain the flexibility to end your contract immediately. To cover this, I suggest including the following sentence in your contract:

> *The provider may terminate this contract at will.*

There are many reasons why you want to make sure that your contract doesn't require you to give the client a termination notice. For example, let's say that your contract requires you to give clients a two-week notice and you are faced with one of the following situations:

- A client is behind in her weekly payments and owes you $450.
- A client notices a bruise on her child's shin and says, "I bet you kicked her there."
- A client threatens to accuse you of child abuse unless you keep her child inside while the other children play outside.
- You suddenly contract a serious illness and must close your program indefinitely.
- You give a client a two-week notice to end your contract, and she becomes disruptive— she starts bad-mouthing you to your other clients, swears in front of the children, and makes a ruckus when she picks up her child.

In all of these situations you need to have the freedom to end your agreement immediately. Without it, the client may be able to enforce your two-week notice requirement against you in court. Some contracts state that

> *The provider may terminate the contract without giving any notice if the client does not make payments when due.*

However, this language limits your possible reasons for ending the contract immediately. For example, if the misbehaving client above has already paid for her last two weeks, you want to be able to warn her that if her behavior doesn't change you will terminate care immediately and give her a refund for the unused days. This wording wouldn't give you the flexibility to do that.

It is perfectly legal to require your clients to give you a two-week notice for ending the contract and not bind yourself in the same way. You need to be able to protect your business from clients who are disruptive or who threaten to register a complaint against you. If a client says that she is willing to make a commitment to your program but is concerned that you might end the relationship without notice, you can say:

> *I try to make it a practice to give clients a two-week notice if I need to end a con-tract. In the many years I have been providing care I have failed to give that notice only once or twice in extreme situations. I can't promise to give you a two-week notice, but I will do my best.*

Most providers find that this kind of statement is enough to reassure their clients about their intentions.

If you have collected the two-week final payment in advance (see page 47) and decide to end the contract, you must either offer to provide care for the last two weeks or refund the client's deposit. It's unfair to keep the deposit if you aren't willing to provide the care.

If you decide to temporarily shut down your business for several months (for example, for the birth of a child or to recover from an illness) or permanently (to take another job or to retire), you may wish to give your clients as much advance notice as possible. However, before you give a long advance notice, consider the consequences if your clients were to leave early. One provider who was preparing to shut down her business gave her clients a two-month notice, and they all left within a few weeks.

The Signatures of the Parties to the Contract

A written contract isn't enforceable until it has been signed by all the parties to it—in this case, that means you and your client(s). After the signature, each party should record the date that she signed the contract. Once the contract is signed, make a copy and give it to the client; put the original signed contract in your file for that client. If you don't have access to a copier, ask the client to sign two copies of the contract, one for each of you.

Before the Signature Lines

There are two statements that I suggest you insert before the signature lines in your contract. First, if you have separated your contract from your policies, as I strongly recommend (see pages 25–26), you can have clients affirm that by signing your contract they agree to abide by your policies. Here's an example of the language you might use:

> *By signing this contract, clients indicate that they have read the provider's policies and agree to follow them. The provider reserves the right to make changes to her policies without notice.*

If you prefer, you can say that you will give clients advance notice of any changes to your policies—the statement in Sample Contract 3 in Appendix A shows that option. (Although you aren't required to give notice for policy changes, it's a good business practice.)

You can also put this statement in your policies and have clients sign your policies in addition to your contract. The legal advantage of putting this language in your contract is that you can prove that the client agreed to follow your policies, if she later disputes that point in a court case.

The second clause that I suggest you insert before the signature lines is a statement that you are allowed to enforce your rules selectively (see page 29).

A failure to enforce one or more terms of this contract does not waive the provider's right to enforce any other terms of this contract.

Signing the Contract

Don't sign and copy the contract until your client has signed it. For example, one provider signed her contract and gave it to her client, who took it home. Later the client left, owing her money. However, the provider was unable to enforce the terms of their agreement because she didn't have a copy of the contract, and the client refused to produce it. If a client refuses to sign your contract, it means that you only have a verbal agreement—and verbal agreements are usually very difficult to enforce in court (see page 21).

Some providers require their clients to sign or initial each page of the contract. This isn't necessary to make the contract terms legally enforceable. However, it may be helpful as a way to ensure that the client understands what he is signing, and it can be useful in resolving conflicts later. One provider had a term in her contract that said, "Client must pay for any excessive damage caused by the child." When a problem arose, the provider had to take the client to court to get paid for the damage; the judge ruled for her, in part because the client's initials were on that page of the contract. Although technically the initials shouldn't have mattered, in this case they did.

Some providers have their contracts notarized, but this isn't necessary either. Having a contract notarized simply means having a notary public certify that she has witnessed the signing of the agreement and has confirmed the identity of the signers. This would only make a difference if you were trying to enforce your contract in court and the other party tried to argue that it wasn't her signature on your contract. Since this is extremely unlikely, it's not worth the time or expense to have your contracts notarized.

Married Parents Should Both Sign the Contract

If the child's parents are married or living together, they should both sign your contract, so that you will be able to enforce the contract with both of them. For example, if the mother signs your contract and one day the father shows up late to pick up the child, you don't want to have an argument with him about paying your late fee. If he has signed the contract, you aren't as likely to have this kind of dispute.

If the child's parents are married or living together and one of them refuses to sign your contract, this could be a warning sign, and you may want to refuse to provide care until the contract has been signed by both parents. You might also want to reconsider whether you want to provide care for this child at all, since this could be a red flag for future problems due to a parent who is uninvolved with the child's care or who decides to challenge the terms of your contract.

Divorced Parents and Custody Issues

If the child's parents are separated, divorced, or never married and living apart, the situation is more complex, especially if custody issues are involved. As a rule, you should ask every new client who is a single parent whether there is a court-ordered custody agreement or restraining order in effect. (In the case of a divorced client, there will always be a custody agreement.) If there is, require the client to give you a copy before you sign a contract, since that is the only way to ensure that the client has the legal authority to represent the child and sign your contract.

There are two kinds of custody, legal and physical. Basically, legal custody means that the person has the right to sign a contract for child care, and physical custody means that the person lives with the child and is responsible for the child's physical well-being. Both kinds of custody may also be shared by the parents. (For more on child custody, see the *Legal and Insurance Guide*.)

If one parent has full legal and physical custody of the child, then he or she is the only person who can legally enter into a contract for the care of the child. The noncustodial parent has no rights and shouldn't be a party to your contract.

If the parents are divorced and they share legal and physical custody, then they should both sign your contract—however, this can lead to difficult situations. Typically, one parent, usually the mother, will approach you to care for the child, but the father is providing some of the money to pay for child care. The parents may or may not be on good terms. The father may or may not be taking the child to and from your care.

Regardless of the circumstances, you should try to get both parents to sign your contract, if at all possible; this will make it easier to enforce your contract and your policies. If one of them refuses to sign, you could insist on it and make it a condition of providing care for the child. Or you could provide care but make it clear to both parents that you will be enforcing all your rules, and if you decide that there are any problems, you will end the agreement.

If the parents share legal custody but the mother has sole physical custody, be aware that this kind of situation can lead to conflicts. In this case, the children live exclusively with the mother but the father has the right to be involved in any decisions about their welfare. In this case, usually the mother will sign your child care contract and the father won't. (The father shouldn't sign the contract unless he is making payments directly to you.)

If any conflicts arise later between the mother and the father, you may find yourself in the middle. For example, the father might ask you for the child's medical records from your files, or he might ask you how much the mother has paid for child care. In this situation, the best advice is to tell the mother that she needs to resolve her conflict with the father without involving you. You can add that if she can't do that, then you may have to stop providing care for the child.

If Your Client Is a Minor

A written contract may not be enforceable if your client is a minor (under the age of eighteen). If you are entering into a contract with a client who is a minor, tell her that she will need to have an adult relative or friend co-sign the contract with her. Make sure that they both understand that if the client doesn't pay you for care under the terms of the contract, her co-signer will be responsible for paying that debt.

If You Work with a Partner

If you are working in partnership with another provider, then you both need to sign the contract for every client. Because of the greater potential for misunderstanding when there are two people involved in running the business, you and your partner will need to make a special effort to communicate clearly with your clients about rules and responsibilities. One way to do this is to put all your communications with clients in writing.

If You Have Employees

If you have an employee or an unpaid assistant who helps you care for the children, that person shouldn't be a party to the contract. However, if you have an employee, you should disclose this to a client before she signs your contract. One way to do this is to introduce your employee to prospective clients when they first meet with you (see page 97). You should also explain your employee's responsibilities—including when (if ever) she will be left alone with the children—in your policies. To reduce the chances of misunderstanding, ask your clients to communicate directly with you rather than through your employee.

CHAPTER FIVE

Terms of Payment

Chapter Summary
This chapter discusses your options for terms of payment and the language
you can use to make sure that those terms are clearly described in your contract. This is the most important part of your contract, and there are many
issues to consider.

In this chapter I will review all the issues related to money—such as your rates, fees, and
terms of payment—that you should consider in writing your contract. I will also discuss the
important issue of the trade-off between time and money.

Setting Your Rates

You can set the regular rate for your services by the month, week, day, or hour. Twenty years
ago child care providers commonly charged by the hour, but this is slowly changing; in most
urban communities they now charge primarily by the week. In many rural communities most
providers still charge by the day or hour. However, as the professionalism of family child
care has grown, more providers have started charging for larger blocks of time, even when
the child is absent, in order to maintain a successful business.

If you would like to set rates for different blocks of time (such as by the hour, day, or
week), the basic guideline is that the smaller the block of your time, the higher your rate
should be. In other words, clients who want part-time care should have to pay more, on an
hourly basis, than those who want full-time care.

For example, let's say that you usually charge $120 a week for 55 hours of care; in this
case, your full-time "regular" rate would be $120 per week. However, you also have drop-in
clients who pay on a daily or hourly basis—how much more should those clients pay than
your regular clients?

If your daily rate were equivalent to your weekly rate, it would be $24 ($120 ÷ 5 = $24);
however, I recommend that you charge at least 40% of your weekly rate per day—and in this
case, that would mean at least $30 per day ($120 x 20% = $30). In the same vein, if your
hourly rate were equivalent to your weekly rate, it would be be $2.18 per hour ($120 ÷ 55

hours = $2.18). However, I recommend that your hourly rate be about 3% of your weekly rate, or $3.60 in this example ($120 x 3% = $3.60).

••

Fees or Tuition?

Some family child care providers use the language of education in their contract and policies. This can include referring to the provider as a "teacher," describing the program as a place where children "learn" and "graduate," and referring to the fees as "tuition." Although this kind of language isn't for everyone, if you are comfortable with it, it can be a way to give your program a more professional image.

••

Before you set your rates, you may want to research the family child care rates in your area—see chapter 10 for a discussion of how to do that. When you do that, bear in mind that many providers undercharge for their services. So if you believe that you are offering high-quality care, you should set your rates in the top 10%–20% of the family child care rates in your area.

You may also want to write your policies before you finalize your rates. Once you make a list of all the services you will be offering, you may realize that you should charge more for your program. (For more information about how to set your rates, see the *Family Child Care Marketing Guide*.)

••

Q & A: Different Rates for Different Clients

Q: Can I charge different rates to different clients?

A: Yes, as long as you don't base your rates on any of the criteria protected by law, which include race, color, sex, disability, religion, and national origin. As long as you don't discriminate on those grounds, you are free to set your rates as you wish for new and existing clients and for different age groups. (For more information on the discrimination laws, see page 75 and the *Legal and Insurance Guide*.)

For example, you can charge less to lower-income clients, and you can charge more to new clients to keep your rates low for your current clients. In most states you can charge private pay clients more than government-subsidized clients but no less than them (ask your county subsidy program for more information). You can also lower your rates on a temporary basis for a client who is having a financial crisis or a family emergency.

••

Family Discounts

Child care can be expensive for large families, and a client who has more than one child in your care may ask whether you offer a family discount. Some family child care providers do offer such discounts (typically 10%–25%), because they want to attract families who will provide significant income each week. Other providers don't offer these discounts, because there are no cost savings in caring for more than one child from the same family. Another option is to offer prospective clients a family discount for a limited time, such as the first six months, to encourage them to try your program. The idea is that by that point they will see what a good job you are doing and be reluctant to switch caregivers.

• •

Photocopy the Payments

It's helpful to photocopy at least one check from each of your clients so that you have a record of the client's bank and account number. (If a client pays you from different bank accounts, copy at least one check from each account.) Having copies of your clients' checks can make it easier to settle disputes and will be necessary if you ever need to collect money from the client after a court ruling (see page 139).

• •

Raising Your Rates

Many family child care providers find it difficult to raise their rates, especially for their existing clients. Some start new clients at a higher rate to avoid raising the rates of their current clients. One way to make it less stressful to raise your rates is to include a rate increase schedule in your contract; for example:

- *The weekly rate will go up 4% each year on the anniversary of signing this contract.*

- *The weekly rate will go up $15 each year on January 1.*

It is usually easier on both you and your clients to raise your rates gradually each year rather than ask for a big increase more rarely and irregularly. You can raise everyone's rates at the same time or you can stagger the increases to minimize your risk in case the new rate causes more than one client to decide to leave your care. The most common times to raise rates are the contract anniversary, the beginning of September, and the beginning of the year. (See chapter 10 for more information about raising your rates.)

Reducing Your Rates for Special Circumstances

Some family child care providers are also willing to reduce their rates if a client's financial situation deteriorates due to divorce, the loss of a job, a death in the family, or a family illness. Others will give free days or discounts to clients who have a history of paying on time. However, I don't recommend that you describe these options in your contract or policies. It's best to keep these options informal to give you greater flexibility in responding to each situation that arises.

Also, any time you charge different rates to different clients you should assume that your other clients will eventually find out about it. Therefore, make sure that you have a logical reason for lowering your rates, in case you have to explain it later. If a client asks you why another client is paying a reduced fee, you can reply,

> *This family has special circumstances that I am helping them with. If your family had similar special circumstances, I would offer you a similar arrangement.*

If you do say something like this, bear in mind that you shouldn't provide any details about these "special circumstances"; if you do, it will violate the first client's privacy, and she will be understandably angry with you when she finds out.

Require Payment in Advance

Now we come to the most important suggestion in this book. I strongly recommend that your contract include the following requirements:

- *The client will pay for child care one week in advance.*

- *The client will pay for the last two weeks of child care upon signing the contract.*

You should put the first of these requirements in the terms of payment section of your contract. I have put the second requirement in the termination section of the sample contract and CD worksheets. However, I will discuss them together since they raise similar issues.

If you include these stipulations in your contract, your new clients will need to pay you for three weeks of care at the time they sign your contract. You can switch your existing clients to paying one week in advance and ask them to give you a deposit for the final two weeks of care by revising their contracts (as explained below).

Although you don't need to put this money in the bank, you won't have the extra security that this money represents unless you save it for the time it is designated for. (You must report advance payments as income on your tax return in the year that you receive them.)

Why Require Clients to Pay One Week in Advance?

A growing number of family child care providers are changing their contracts to require all their clients to pay in advance—some even require a month's payment in advance. There are many reasons to require at least one week's payment in advance:

- Your clients are used to paying for most services before they receive them. Renters pay the landlord at the beginning of the month. The fees for services (such as cell phone service), subscriptions (such as magazines), and memberships (such as health clubs) are all due before you receive the service. Also, most child care centers charge in advance.

- Since you have expenses throughout the week (for food, gas, supplies, etc.), you will be subsidizing your clients if you wait to collect your fees until the end of the week.

- You will lose income if a client who normally pays at the end of the week walks out with his child in the middle of a week and refuses to pay for the last half-week of care. If you and a client have an argument over money, you are better off having the money in hand than trying to collect it from the client.

How to Switch Your Existing Clients to Advance Payments

If you would like to switch your existing clients to paying in advance, here's how to make the change. Let's say that your clients are currently paying you on Friday for the week that is ending. First, give them a month or two advance notice that you will be changing your contract. Revise your contract by adding language such as the following:

Fees are due on Friday each week for the next week of care.

Inform your clients that in order to meet this requirement, on one particular Friday (specify the date) an extra week's payment will be due. After that, they will go back to paying your regular rate on Friday, as before.

If a client normally pays you by the hour or day and the amount paid varies from week to week, review the client's payments for the last several months and determine the average amount the client has paid you per week. Then tell the client that he will need to pay you that amount in addition to his actual weekly fee on the date that the advance payment is due.

If one of your clients finds it difficult to pay you the double amount in one week, add an addendum to that client's contract saying he will pay you a little extra each week until he has paid in full for the final week of care:

Client agrees to pay an extra $10 a week for twelve weeks until one week of child care has been paid in advance.

You can accept partial payments for any reasonable number of weeks to accommodate a client who is in financial difficulty. If a client receives a county or state child care subsidy and also gives you a co-payment, you can ask the client to pay you one week's co-payment in advance. (But first, check with the subsidy program to make sure that is allowed.)

Require a Deposit for the Last Two Weeks

One of the most common complaints I hear from providers is that although their contract requires clients to pay for the two-week notice period, many clients leave without paying for it. Although you can always sue the client, it may be difficult to recover the money. The solution to this problem is to require your clients to pay you for the last two weeks of care when they first enroll or the next time you renew their contract. (If the client can't afford to pay the entire deposit at one time, you can set up a payment plan to collect the money.)

For example, Sample Contract 3 includes the following language in the termination section of the contract:

Client will pay $270 at the time of signing the contract; this deposit will pay for the client's last two weeks of care, even if the provider's rates are raised later.

If you have a subsidized client who is also giving you a co-payment, I recommend that you require her to pay the last two weeks' co-payment in advance (but first make sure that the subsidy program allows this). If she can't afford to pay all at once, set up a payment plan of a few dollars a week that will allow her to come into compliance with your rules.

When a client decides to leave your program, remind him that he doesn't have to give you any money for the last two weeks, because he has already paid for that time. (He doesn't get a refund if he leaves before the two weeks are over.)

You should give the client a full two weeks of child care in return for his deposit, even if your rates have gone up since you signed the contract. If you just apply the deposit as a partial payment for the last two weeks, then you may have to pay interest on the client's money for the time you have held it. Since this isn't worth doing, specify instead that the deposit entitles the client to the final two weeks of care, regardless of its cost at that time. (If you're worried that you'll lose money when your rates go up, remember that you will be holding the deposits for months, if not years, and during that time you'll be earning interest on the money.)

• •

The Two Most Important Rules to Put in Your Contract

Client will pay at least one week in advance.
Client will pay in advance for the last two weeks of care.

If you enforce these two rules, you will completely avoid the two most common money problems that providers have with clients. Your clients won't leave owing you money, and you will never have to sue a client for an unpaid bill. These rules are reasonable and affordable; you can allow clients to pay a little extra each week over time. Although it may be more difficult to introduce these rules if the other providers in your area aren't following them, if you offer high-quality child care you shouldn't have any trouble making this change.

• •

Getting a deposit for the last two weeks of care also gives you more control if you are the one who decides to end the relationship. For example, let's say that you tell a client you will be ending his contract but will continue providing care for another two weeks to give him some time to find a new provider. He may react badly to this news, even if you handle it professionally and he has never had any complaints about you before. He may feel that you are rejecting his child and he may not want to leave her in your care anymore. In many cases like this, the client decides to leave immediately. If you haven't collected the two-week advance payment from him, it may be difficult to get him to pay you for those weeks.

Requiring advance payment for the last two weeks gives you more confidence as well as financial security and peace of mind. You may be reluctant to enforce your rules if you are afraid that your clients will leave owing you money. Without this fear, you can be more assertive about enforcing your rules—and as a result you'll probably have fewer conflicts with clients.

• •

Do You Need to Pay Interest on Client Deposits?

If your policy is that the final deposit will entitle the client to the final two weeks of care (regardless of its actual cost at that time), rather than be applied toward the actual cost of the final two weeks of care, then you don't need to give the client interest on the money. Otherwise, you do.

• •

Payment Due Date

It isn't enough to specify your rates in your contract; you also need to clearly indicate when the payments are due. Be specific about the day and time of day:

* *Fees are due at pickup time on Friday for the next week.*

* *Fees are due at drop-off time on Monday for the next week.*

Most providers find it easiest to have all clients pay on the same day, whether the payments are weekly, semi-weekly, or monthly. This method involves less paperwork and fewer trips to the bank.

One way to make sure that you get paid on time is to ask your clients who pay weekly to give you a set of postdated checks at the beginning of the month. For example, if the client pays you every Monday, ask her to give you four checks for the amount of your weekly fee dated for each Monday in the month. This can be an effective way to deal with clients who tend to forget their checkbook or run out of checks on payday. One provider insisted that a client who had forgotten her checkbook go to the ATM and return with the money. Although the client got mad, she did as she was told. After she got home she cooled off—and the next day she sent the provider a bouquet of flowers with an apology.

Use an Automatic Payment Plan

There are two ways to do an automatic payment plan. You can sign a direct deposit agreement with your client and use a direct deposit service to electronically transfer money from the client's checking account to your bank account on the payment due date. For example, one company that offers this service is Reliafund (www.reliafund.com).

However, the client may prefer to simply ask her bank to automatically deposit money into your account on a regular schedule. In this case she will have control over the deposits and will be able to cancel them at any time. If you use this approach, your contract should require her to give you written advance notice before cancelling the automatic deposits:

The client agrees to participate in an automatic payment plan. The client will ask her bank to automatically deposit $150 into the provider's bank account every Friday to pay for the next week of care. If the client chooses to discontinue this service, she must notify the provider in writing one week in advance.

Consider Accepting Credit Cards

For years many child care centers have accepted credit cards as payment for child care services. Family child care providers have generally not done so because of the extra cost and paperwork involved. Credit card companies normally charge about 2.5% to process a credit card payment, and there are also additional bank fees involved. However, with the growing use of credit cards in all aspects of daily life, this may be something to consider. The benefits may include more reliable payments and fewer late payments. (Credit card payments are less likely to bounce than checks, because banks pay credit card bills first.) To start taking credit cards, go to your bank and ask them to set it up for you.

• •

Bounced Check Fee

Some family child care providers include a term in their contract stating that they will charge a fee for a bounced check, like any other business:

The fee for an insufficient funds check will be $ _____, plus any bank charges to the provider's account.

• •

Late Payment Fees

I recommend that you charge a late fee when a client doesn't pay you on time—and if you do so, you need to describe that fee in your contract. Many providers charge a fee of $5 or $10 per day for late payments. You could also refuse to provide care until the client pays you. For example, if a client doesn't pay you on Friday for the next week, tell the client that you won't accept her child on Monday unless you receive the payment that morning.

Will a Court Enforce Your Late Fee?

If your fee for a late payment is $5 a day and a client leaves without giving you the two-week advance notice required under your contract, the late fees can add up to hundreds of dollars by the time you appear in small-claims court to try to recover the money for the two weeks. In this situation, the court probably won't require the client to pay the late fees, even if you win the battle over the two-week notice. Judges are unlikely to award late fees that they consider to be excessive. This doesn't mean that you shouldn't charge late fees; it just means you can't necessarily expect to recover them in a lawsuit.

Some judges have told providers that late fees are illegal, but this probably isn't accurate. Usually what the judge means is that state laws prevent you from charging excessive interest on debt (usury). Although state laws vary, late fees should not be treated in the same way as interest because the services provided are not based on a loan.

Early Drop-off and Late Pickup Fees

Family child care providers work very long hours. A national survey indicates that providers care for children an average of eleven hours a day, or fifty-five hours a week. When you are working that many hours, it can be very frustrating when a client drops off her children early or arrives late to pick them up. There are several ways to deal with these problems. First of all, your contract needs to state the hours that are covered by your regular fee so that it will be clear when the client is arriving early or late (see chapter 4).

The most common way to deal with these situations is to charge a late (or early) fee; it just makes sense to charge for all the time that you are working. Some providers give their clients a ten- or fifteen-minute grace period at pickup time before charging the late fee; others offer no grace period at all. I've even seen a contract that states that any client who is ever late to pick up a child will be immediately terminated. (Although that's a rather drastic step, it has solved the problem—the provider told me that none of her clients have ever been late.)

Time versus Money

Some providers include a late fee or other consequences in their contract but feel uncomfortable about enforcing those provisions. To help resolve this inner conflict, consider this question: Which is more important to you—time or money?

If time is more important to you than money, this means that you don't want to work later than your regular hours, no matter how much a client pays you. You want the time to spend with your family or by yourself. In this case, you will need to set a consequence that is high enough to stop late pickups. That might mean charging a late fee of $1 a minute, or more if necessary. One provider complained to me that one client kept showing up late, even though she was being charged a late fee of $50 per half-hour. Since the client didn't hesitate to pay the late fee, I told the provider that she would need to raise her late fee even more if she wanted to change that client's behavior.

If money is more important to you than time, this means that you would be willing to work later than your regular hours for the right amount of money. In this case, you should set your late fee low enough that some of your clients can afford to be late and you can earn some extra money. The specific amount will depend on the financial circumstances of your clients, and you may need to experiment a bit to get it right.

For example, let's say that you're charging a late fee of $1 per minute ($60 an hour) and you're finding that most of your clients are arriving on time since they aren't willing to pay this. If you lower your late fee to $.50 a minute ($30 an hour) you may find that more of them feel as if they can afford to be late. It's easier to lower the rate than to raise it, and if you'd like to try a lower rate on a temporary basis, you can tell your clients that you're having a "sale" on late fees.

There's also another way to approach this problem. One provider told me that she didn't like to charge a "late fee" because that term was associated with guilt and created tension between her and her clients. Instead, after her regular pickup time she started charging an "evening rate" that was higher than her regular rate. She said that calling it an evening rate instead of a late fee reduced the stress on both her and her clients. This is another solution that you could try if money is more important to you than time.

Another provider who offers child care in a building separate from her home asked me what to do about a client who was regularly late without giving her any advance notice. She said that she would often have to sit alone with the child for an hour or more waiting for him to show up. In a situation like this, where you are greatly inconvenienced, you have several options:

- You could charge an extremely high late fee.
- You could charge your usual late fee and bring the child home with you. (You would need to get the client's written permission first.)
- If the client won't change his behavior, you could terminate care.

Sample Contract Language

Once you have decided whether time or money is more important to you and what consequences you will set for clients who don't arrive on time, you need to put those provisions in writing and add them to your contract. The CD includes several examples of the kinds of language you can put in your contract to define those consequences:

- *The client will pay an additional fee of $1.00 per minute if the child is dropped off earlier or picked up later than the time stipulated in this contract.*

- *If the client notifies the provider of an early drop-off the night before, there will be no early drop-off fee.*

- *If the client notifies the provider of a late pickup at least one hour before the scheduled pickup time, there will be no late pickup fee.*

- *The client will be allowed to drop off early or pick up late six times per calendar year without charge. After that, there will be a fee of $1.00 per minute for all early drop-offs and late pickups.*

- *The client will be allowed to drop off early or pick up late 10 times per calendar year without charge. If there are any more early drop-offs or late pickups after that, the provider will terminate this child care agreement.*

- *The provider is willing to provide care after the client's regular pickup time of 6:00 PM. After that time the child care rate will be $.50 per minute.*

- *All fees for early drop-off and late pickup are due at the end of that day of care.*

- *If the client fails to pick up the child by 6:00 PM, the provider will terminate the child care agreement.*

- *If the client fails to pick up the child by 6:00 PM, the provider may choose to have another caregiver take the child.*

For the last option, you will need to have the clients sign an agreement in advance that specifies the other caregivers who are allowed to pick up the child; this might be another child care provider, a family friend, a neighbor, or any other person the client authorizes to pick up the child.

Holidays, Vacations, and Absences

It's important for your contract to clarify how you will handle holidays, vacations, sick days, absences, and other situations when either you aren't available or the client doesn't bring the child to care. These are common situations that often lead to disputes and misunderstanding, so it's important to think them through in advance and explain how you will handle them in your contract.

Holidays

Since most of your clients get several paid holidays from their employers, it isn't unreasonable for you to do so as well. Charging for holidays can help you maintain a regular income, and for some providers that financial stability is necessary to stay in business. The eight federal holidays for which most providers close their business are:

- New Year's Day
- Martin Luther King Day
- Presidents' Day
- Memorial Day
- Independence Day
- Labor Day
- Thanksgiving Day
- Christmas Day

When one of these holidays falls on a weekend, the holiday is either the Friday before it or the Monday after it. In addition to these basic federal holidays, you should consider any other holidays that are important to you, including religious or ethnic holidays (such as Cinco de Mayo, Easter, Eid-al-Fitr, Kwanzaa, or Passover).

If you close for these holidays and haven't been charging your clients for those days, consider adding a few paid holidays to your contract each year. (Some providers do this instead of raising their rates each year.) If you are already charging clients for the eight federal holidays, you can add a few more holidays each year. Here are some other days that you might consider closing your business:

- A full or half day on New Year's Eve day
- Good Friday
- Columbus Day
- Veterans Day
- The day after Thanksgiving
- A full or half day on Christmas Eve day
- Another day at Christmas (usually the day before or after Christmas Day)
- Your birthday
- Your wedding anniversary
- Your personal days off (see below)

If you aren't closed on these days, you could start by closing your business for some of them without charging your clients. Over time you could increase the number of days that you take off and require your clients to pay for some of them, if you feel that is appropriate.

In making the decision about whether to charge for a holiday, consider whether most of your clients are getting it as a paid holiday. Since you shouldn't be getting fewer paid holidays than they are, you could make it a policy to (eventually) charge for every holiday that is a paid holiday for most of your clients.

It's a good idea to send your clients a yearly announcement with the dates of all the days on which your business will be closed during the next year, including any scheduled vacation or personal days (see below). If you do this at the beginning of the year, be sure to include New Year's Day for the following year on the list.

Your Personal Days Off

In addition to holidays, every year there will be some days on which you will either choose to or have to close your business for personal reasons. Like your clients, you need to have paid time off to rest, attend a professional conference, or spend time with your family so that you can return to work refreshed. These days might include your:

- Vacation
- Sick days (personal or family)
- Professional development days
- Maternity or paternity leave

Your contract should clearly spell out the payment plan for your vacations and personal days off. One way to do this is to state in your contract that you will take a specific number of paid personal days each year that you may use for any of the above reasons. Another option is to break down how many paid days you will take for each of the above reasons in your contract.

With the exception of vacation time, most providers don't charge for the days that they are unable to offer care. Some of them do charge for taking professional development days to attend conferences and training workshops, since they can explain to clients that these activities will help improve the quality of their program.

Your Vacation Time

It is becoming increasingly common for family child care providers to charge their clients during the time that the provider takes her own family vacation, usually for one or two weeks. However, it is still true that many providers rarely take a vacation, and if they do, they don't charge their clients for that time. (If you plan to take a vacation, let your clients know as early in the year as you can; see page 54.)

If you are thinking of starting to charge for your vacation time, be aware that some of your clients may complain that they have to pay double for child care while you're gone. Another potential problem is that a client may end her contract just before you plan to leave; if you don't have a deposit for the last two weeks of care (see page 47), you will lose the money you were counting on to help pay for your time off.

One solution is to spread the cost of your vacation time throughout the year. To do this, divide the amount that each client would pay for your vacation weeks by the number of remaining weeks in the year and increase the weekly rate for each client by this amount throughout the year.

For example, if your regular weekly fee is $125, and your contract says that clients must pay for your two-week vacation, divide two weeks of pay ($250) by the number of remaining weeks in the year (50) to get $5. Then raise your rates by $5 a week, and stop charging your clients for your vacation weeks. (If you only took one week of vacation, you would raise your rates by $2.45 a week—$125 divided by 51 weeks.) By doing this, you will be getting the same amount as if you charged for your two-week vacation, and it won't matter if a client leaves your program just before you go on vacation.

If you do raise your rates just to pay for your vacation time, don't tell your clients that this increase will pay for your vacation—just say that your rates are going up. If your clients think of the rate increase as an advance payment on your vacation, a client might ask for a refund if she leaves before you take your vacation.

• •

A Verbal Agreement Won't Amend Your Contract

When you make a change to your contract, you have to put it in writing to make it legally enforceable. A verbal agreement can't change the terms of a written contract. Give the client notice (two weeks, perhaps) that you will be introducing a new contract term, and have them sign a revised version of your contract that contains the new rules. (See page 106 for other ways to make changes to your contract.)

• •

Client Vacations

Just as you should give your clients several weeks' advance notice of the holidays and vacation days on which you will be closed, you should also require your clients to give you several weeks' notice of their vacation plans. Like all the other terms in your contract, it is up to you whether to charge your clients when they go on vacation and the children don't come to your program. The important thing is to make sure that your contract explains the payment plan for client vacations.

If you don't charge for client vacations, your contract should stipulate that your clients can't carry these vacation days forward from one year to another. For example, let's say that your contract allows clients to take one week per year as family vacation time and not pay for that week. If a client only takes three vacation days one year, don't allow her to carry over the remaining two vacation days to the next year.

Raising Your Rates to Cover Vacations and Holidays

As for your vacation time, if you can't bring yourself to charge for holidays and the client's vacation days, consider raising your regular rate to cover this time.

For example, if your program is open five days a week, then the eight federal holidays plus two weeks' vacation (ten child care days) equals eighteen days. With a five-day work week there are 260 working days in a 52-week year, and eighteen days would represent 7% of your total working days ($18 \div 260 = 7\%$). If you normally charge $110 a week for child care, you could raise your rates by 7% to $118 a week ($110 \times 107\% = \$118$), stop charging for two weeks of client vacation and the eight federal holidays, and still receive the same amount of money.

This is also a good way to set your rates to compensate for clients who are teachers and take their children out of your program during the summer.

When a Child Is Sick or Absent

It is a given that the children in your care will sometimes become ill and not be able to attend your program—and when that happens you shouldn't necessarily lose income. You need to decide under what circumstances, if any, you will care for a sick child (see chapter 8), and when you do, whether you want to charge more for doing so. Also, your policies should help to protect the health of the children by encouraging the parents to keep a sick child at home.

Your contract can allow your clients to keep a sick child at home for a specific number of days per year without charge, or it can say that you will continue to charge your normal rate when a child is absent, regardless of the reason for the absence. If you're caring for more than one child in a family, your contract should make it clear whether the unpaid sick days apply to each child individually or whether they can be used by any of the children in the family.

You can also set different rules based on the age of the child. For example, your contract could say that children over the age of two will have four unpaid sick days per year, and children under the age of two will have six unpaid sick days per year. This will help encourage your clients to keep a sick infant at home.

If a child has a long-term illness and uses up all her sick days and other options, you could charge a holding fee to keep the space open until the child can return (see page 57).

Another way to deal with a long illness is to ask the client to continue to pay you only if her employer pays her while she is missing work to care for the child. If you don't charge a client who isn't being paid when caring for a sick child, it might enable her to stay home until the child has fully recovered.

Unnotified Absences

Your contract can require clients to notify you in advance (before the scheduled starting time) whenever a child won't be coming to your program. You want to avoid a situation in which a client doesn't bring his child, doesn't notify you, and then doesn't want to pay for that day because he claims that the child was sick and covered by your sick day policy. If your contract doesn't specifically cover this kind of situation, you probably won't be able to get him to pay you.

To modify your contract so that your clients are required to notify you of all absences in advance, rewrite your contract (or make an addendum to it—see page 106) to require your clients to pay you for absences if they don't notify you before the child is scheduled to arrive that day, regardless of any other terms in your contract.

Here's an example of the language you might use:

> *The client must notify the provider in advance (before the scheduled starting time) whenever a child won't be coming to care due to illness or any other reason. If the client doesn't provide that advance notice, the client will pay for the missed day(s) of care, regardless of any other terms of this contract.*

Next, give your clients advance notice (two weeks, perhaps) and give them a copy of the new policy that you will be implementing. Explain that you need to know in advance whenever a child will be absent so that you can plan your menu and activity schedule.

Have each client sign and date the new contract (or amendment), then sign and date it yourself. If you use an amendment, attach the original signed amendment to the client's contract, and give the client a copy.

Holding Fees

You may run into situations in which a client wants to sign your contract but doesn't want her child to begin your program until weeks or months later. For example, this can happen when a parent is pregnant and wants to reserve a spot in your program before the child is born. Another situation would be a client who is a teacher and wants to stay home with her child in the summer and return him to your program in the fall. You might also have a situation in which a child will be absent for several weeks and his parent would like to hold his place in your program so that he will be able to return later.

How should you respond if you are asked to reserve a space in your program for several weeks or months? I believe that you should offer these clients one of the following two options in your contract:

- *The provider agrees to hold a space in her program until _____ [date] for the client's child. In return for agreeing to hold a space for the child, the client agrees to pay the provider $ ____ per week during the holding period. Payment is due _____ [weekly, bi-weekly, monthly]. If the client decides not to enroll the child before the end of the holding period, the holding fee will not be refundable. The holding fee cannot be applied to care once the child is enrolled.*

- *The client wishes to enroll her child with the provider starting on _____ [date]. However, the client chooses not to pay a holding fee, and the provider does not agree to hold a space for the child. If before the above date the client wishes to hold a spot for the child, the client can request this of the provider. If at that time the provider agrees to hold the spot until the above date, the client will pay the provider $ ____.*

If you promise to hold a space in your program for a future client, you should charge something in return for that promise. How much should you charge? There's no consensus about that. Some providers charge a flat fee, others charge half their normal rate, and others charge their full rate.

If the client isn't willing to pay a holding fee, then you definitely shouldn't promise to hold the space. Also, you shouldn't allow the holding fee to be applied to the cost of child care once the child is enrolled in your program. The purpose of the holding fee is to compensate you for holding the space open and turning down the opportunity to make money by enrolling other clients. If you apply the holding fee to the cost of care once the child is enrolled, you have given something for nothing.

I have heard of many cases where a provider promised to hold a space without a holding fee and turned away other paying clients, and then the client decided at the last minute not to enroll her child after all. The potential for a significant financial loss is too great not to charge for promising to hold the spot. If the client doesn't enroll the child as agreed, the holding fee will help reimburse you for the time and money that you lost keeping the space open. A client who is unwilling to pay a holding fee shouldn't expect you to make any promises.

Charging a holding fee can help you avoid problems such as this one: The mother of a newborn baby signed a contract with a provider and paid a $300 deposit for the first and last weeks of child care that was scheduled to begin several months later. However, when the time came, the client changed her mind and demanded her money back. She argued that because there had been no first or last week of care, her money should be refunded.

The provider could have prevented this problem from arising by charging a holding fee rather than accepting a deposit so far in the future (if you do this, be sure to state in the contract that the holding fee isn't refundable and can't be applied toward child care services once the child is enrolled).

Another problem in the above example is that the agreement didn't spell out when the child care would begin, which allowed the client to argue that she shouldn't have to pay for care that had never begun. To avoid this problem, always put a starting date in your contracts (see page 35). If you don't know exactly when the starting date will be (as in the case of a newborn baby), put in an estimated starting date. You can also state that if the client changes her mind and wants a refund, she must notify you at least two weeks before that starting date. This will give you some time to make other arrangements.

You Don't Have to Charge a Holding Fee

There are also situations in which you might not want to charge a holding fee or might want to charge less than usual, such as:

- A low-income client wants you to hold a space in your program. She agrees to pay your holding fee, and you tell her that you will refund her holding fee by any amount that you earn caring for children on a temporary basis during the holding period.

- You promise to hold a space without a fee for one of your current clients who is pregnant. This might be the best course when you want to make sure that the family stays with you and you don't really want to fill the spot with a child from another family.

- A client is laid off from work (or loses a job or suffers a serious illness) and has to temporarily remove her child from your care. In this case you might not want to charge a fee to hold her child's place in your program, if you can afford not to. However, set a time when the holding period will expire and renegotiate it with the client at that time. You don't want to promise to hold a space open for an indefinite period of time.

Other Fees

Since all your terms about time and money need to be in your contract, your contract also needs to include any other fees that you might apply, and it has to explain in what situations the client would be liable for paying those fees. The possibilities for additional fees include (but aren't limited to) the following kinds of charges.

Registration/Enrollment Fee

Many child care centers charge a registration fee to help cover the cost of client interviews and the paperwork associated with enrolling a new child or re-enrolling a current child. You may also want to consider charging such a fee. Also, if you review and update your contract and policies once a year, you might charge a re-enrollment fee of $25 or so to help cover the cost of the time you spend rewriting your agreements and meeting with your clients to go over the changes.

License and Inspection Fee

A growing number of states are requiring family child care providers to pay a licensing or inspection fee. If you have to pay such a fee, you can pass on the cost of the fee to your clients. When the fee is due, simply divide the amount that you have to pay by the number of clients you have and add it to their next bill.

Business Liability Insurance Fee

All family child care providers should buy professional business liability insurance to protect themselves from the risks of running a business out of their home. Because this insurance protects your clients as well, you may want to pass on some of the cost to them. You can add a few dollars to each client's bill when your insurance premiums come due (usually twice a year), or raise your regular rates to cover the annual cost. Explain to your clients that they can have more peace of mind because your business is covered by adequate business liability insurance.

Field Trip Fees

If you take the children in your care on a lot of field trips to the zoo, museums, or other locations where there are extra costs involved, you may want to charge a small field trip fee. However, don't charge a transportation fee based on the fact that you are transporting the children in your car—if you do, your car insurance company will probably require you to purchase commercial vehicle insurance, which is very expensive.

If some of your clients are using their cars to transport the children on field trips, be sure that those clients have a current driver's license and adequate car insurance. Also, be sure to bring along the emergency contact information for all the children (the phone numbers for their parents) on every field trip. (For more on the legal and insurance aspects of transporting the children in your care, see the *Legal and Insurance Guide*.)

• •

Don't Put Your Policy Number in Your Contract

Although you can state in your contract that you carry business liability insurance, I don't recommend that you identify your insurance company or provide your policy number. If a client decides to make a claim against your liability insurance policy because her child was injured in your care, you want to find out about it first (when she asks you for your insurance information). At that point, tell her that you need to talk to your insurance agent and will get back to her. Then ask your insurance agent how to proceed.

• •

Fees for Extra Services

You could also charge additional fees to cover the cost of optional or extra services or programs, such as toilet training, a diaper service, disposable diapers, a children's curriculum, swimming lessons, ballet lessons, or other classes.

If a client asks you to do extra services—such as washing a child's clothes, cutting a child's hair, making an early breakfast, or preparing a take-home dinner—you have three options: refuse to do the service, do the service and charge extra for it, or do the service without charging extra for it. If a client expects you to perform these services without compensation, you can point out that your contract doesn't require you to do that. Another option is to ask the client to do a favor for you in return for your extra services (such as bringing some extra toys, helping you on a field trip, or providing her professional expertise to you).

If you don't know what to charge for a service, you could ask the client what she would be willing to pay you for it. You could also contact local child care centers to see how much they charge for that service. (If you do that, don't identify yourself as a family child care provider, since it's illegal to discuss rates with a competitor—see the *Legal and Insurance Guide*.) You could also ask your local child care resource and referral agency for advice.

• •

If You Barter Your Services

Some providers make barter arrangements with their clients—instead of money, they accept other products and services in exchange for child care. For example, I know of providers who have exchanged child care for new windows, car repairs, chiropractic care, and riding lessons for their children. When you agree to barter your services, you should describe that agreement in a contract, just like paying with cash. Your contract should spell out exactly what services are being exchanged:

One week of child care in exchange for installing four new windows.

Even though you don't receive any money, bartering doesn't allow you to pay less in taxes. You must report as income the amount that you would have received if the client had paid cash for the child care that you bartered. For more information on bartering, see the *Family Child Care Record-Keeping Guide*.

• •

Charging for Food

You may also wish to charge for meals—or for special foods, such as baby food and formula. Instead of charging a fee, you could also give your clients the option of bringing their own food or baby formula. You could also ask them to bring a special snack or treat to help you reduce your food expenses. However, bear in mind that you can't charge for any food that is reimbursed by the Food Program. (Check with your Food Program sponsor to see if there are any rules about clients who bring their own food.)

Charging for Damage by the Child

If you've been a family child care provider for a while, you know that the children will inevitably damage your property. The damage might be minor, such as breaking a glass or a toy or staining your carpets and furniture. However, the expense could be significant if you end up having to replace furniture or other costly household items.

If a client has homeowners insurance, her policy will usually cover any significant damage that her child causes to your property. If the cost of the damage is significant, ask the client to find out whether her insurance will cover it. If her insurance has a high deductible, you could choose to share the cost with her.

Since it usually isn't advisable to submit an insurance claim for just a few hundred dollars, some providers don't ask clients to pay for minor damages. However, you could ask the client to replace the item. Also, you may want to hold the client responsible regardless of the cost if the child has deliberately damaged or misused an item. If the client doesn't have homeowners insurance, she may just have to pay you out of her own pocket.

PART III

Writing Your Policies

CHAPTER SIX

What Should Be in Your Policies?

Chapter Summary
This chapter introduces the five key areas that you may want to consider covering in your policy handbook. It also describes how you can use the policy worksheets and the sample policy handbook on the CD to create your own policies.

To communicate most clearly with your clients, you will need a written set of policies as well as a written contract. We have seen that your contract contains the legally enforceable terms of your business relationship with your clients. Your policies are the rules, procedures, and forms that tell them how you will run your business and care for children. Your policies might cover a wide range of topics—your philosophy of child care, the activities in your program, how you will discipline, transport, and toilet-train the children, and much more.

• •

You Can Create a Client Policy Handbook
To make your policies easy to consult, you can put them in a policy handbook for your clients. Although this is optional, it will be helpful to both you and your clients to have all your policies in one document. A dated handbook also makes it easier to communicate and keep track of changes when you update your rules. In this book I will discuss the contents of your policies, rather than how you provide them to clients. So when I use the term "policy handbook," I simply mean your complete set of policies, regardless of how you organize them or present them to clients.

• •

Some providers have many policies and forms; others have only a few. It's up to you to decide how much is enough. I have seen some policy handbooks that are two pages long and others that are forty-five pages long. You can choose to include (or omit) a policy on any topic. Since it is your business, as a rule you are allowed to set your policies as you wish, with few legal restrictions.

• •

Your State May Regulate the Terms in Your Contract or Policies
Some states have regulations that require you to use specific forms or to include certain terms in your client agreement—and those requirements may be different from the recommendations in this book. For example, your state may require that you cover your illness policy in your contract, while I recommend that you cover it in your policies. You should ask your licensor if there are any specific terms or topics that you are required to include in your contract or policies.

• •

The Key Elements of Your Policies

Although there are no requirements about what you have to include in your policies, there are five key topics that I recommend you consider covering in your policies:

1. Provider information
2. Client responsibilities
3. Child care program
4. Illness, health, and safety policies
5. Policies for transporting the children

You don't need to include all five elements or organize them like this; this order is just a suggestion. I will discuss the first two topics in chapter 7 and the next three topics in chapter 8. In those chapters I will cover the policy issues that are important for most providers to consider, but you may also want to add other policies that aren't covered there. You are free to set any policies you wish for your business, as long as you don't violate the law.

If your business is relatively new, you may not be sure what your policies should be. For example, you may wonder whether to ask your clients to bring presents for each child's birthday, because you are concerned that it might be a financial burden for some of them. If you aren't sure what your policy should be in a certain area, it's best omit it from your handbook until you have decided. It is better to have no written policy than one that you don't follow (see page 117). You can start with the policies that make sense to you now, and add more rules as you gain experience.

Forms

It's helpful to include all the forms that you use in your program—such as your enrollment form, field trip permission form, and consent to give a child medication—in a separate section at the end of your policies. This will make it easy for your clients to find and copy a form, fill it out, and bring it to you when needed.

The Sample Policy Handbook in Appendix B

Appendix B of this book provides a sample policy handbook that you can use as a model of what your policies might look like (although you might choose very different policies from those shown in the sample). The CD that comes with this book includes policy worksheets and forms that you can use to assemble your own policy handbook. The worksheets include a comprehensive list of policy options that you can choose from, including all the language shown in the examples in this book.

You can save the policy worksheets on the CD to your own computer and then edit them as you like. The electronic format will make it easy to select the policy options you want and to make changes as your program evolves.

• •

Other Sample Contracts and Policies

If you'd like to see other sample contracts and policies, you may want to contact:

- Other family child care providers
- Your child care licensor
- Your local child care resource and referral agency
- Your local family child care association
- Your Food Program sponsor

You can also find more samples on the Internet; a growing number of family child care providers have Web sites, and they often post their contracts and policies online. For a list of links to family child care sites, visit www.redleafinstitute.org.

• •

Discuss Your Policies with Your Clients

For your policies and forms to be effective, you will need to take the time to carefully review them with each new client before you begin caring for the child. Some policies—such as the procedures you will use to help a child learn to use the toilet or how you will care for a child with special needs—will require consultation with the individual client. Other policies, such as your illness policy or your activity, meal, and nap schedules, may not be as negotiable. (The forms that you ask your clients to sign shouldn't be subject to negotiation; the parent either signs the form, or doesn't.)

Some of your policies may be flexible based upon the needs of the individual child. For example, you might say to a new client, "When would you like Janesha to take a nap each day? I prefer between 1:00 and 2:00 in the afternoon, but I'm flexible." On the other hand, if you have an established routine that you don't want to disrupt, you might say, "I don't feed breakfast to the other children in my care, and it would be disruptive if I only fed Janesha. So I'd appreciate it if you would give her breakfast before she arrives at my program in the morning."

When discussing your policies with your clients, be clear about what is negotiable and what isn't. If you have said that a policy isn't negotiable, it isn't a good idea to compromise it for one client or "just this once" unless you have a good reason for doing so, since your other clients are likely to hear about it and complain. (For more information about negotiating exceptions to your policies, see chapter 10.)

• •

Choose the Policies That Make Sense for Your Business

In the next two chapters I will explain a range of policy options and make some recommendations about them. However, bear in mind that there are very few legal requirements about what you put in your policies—as a rule you are free to write and organize your policies as you wish. This means that you don't have to follow any of the recommendations in this book that don't seem right for your program.

• •

Making Changes to Your Policies

Like your contract, you should review your policies and forms at least once a year to see if you need to make any changes (see chapter 10 for a discussion of making changes to your contracts and policies). If you have separated your contract from your policies as I recommend (see pages 25–26), then you can change your policies or add a new one at any time. If not, you will need to rewrite your contract and convince all your clients to sign the new agreement before you can implement a new policy. If you like, you can require yourself to give clients advance notice before you make any changes to your policies:

> *I will give you a two-week written notice before revising my current policies or adding new policies.*

Should Your Clients Sign Your Policies?

Although you don't need to have your clients sign your policies, many providers like to reinforce the seriousness of their rules by asking their clients to sign a statement, such as the following, on a page at the end of their policy handbook:

> *By signing this page, you indicate that you have read my policies and agree to follow them. I reserve the right to make changes to my policies without notice.*

As described on pages 39–40, you can also put this kind of language in your contract, and this may help you in court if a client claims that she never agreed to follow your policies. However, other than that, the benefit of asking your clients to sign your policies is mostly psychological. With that in mind, there are basically three places that you could ask your clients to sign to reinforce the importance of your rules:

1. You can ask your clients to sign a statement at the end of your policy handbook stating that they have read your policies and will abide by them (as shown above).
2. You can put a statement in your contract that the client's signature indicates that she agrees to follow your policies (as shown on page 39).
3. You can ask your clients to sign or initial every page of your policies to indicate that they have read the rules on that page and will abide by them.

You are free to use any or all of the above approaches to reinforce the importance of your policies. However, bear in mind that these signatures don't mean that you can legally force a client to comply with a policy. If a client refuses to follow one of your policies, your ultimate recourse is usually to just terminate her contract.

CHAPTER SEVEN

You and Your Client

Chapter Summary
This chapter discusses in detail the policy topics that provide general information about you, your program, and your client—provider information and client responsibilities.

In addition to explaining your rules, your policy handbook is also a marketing tool; when prospective clients are considering your program, they are likely to examine your policies closely for clues about what kind of person you are and whether their child will be happy in your care. The first two elements to consider for your policy handbook, provider information and client responsibilities, give you an opportunity to introduce yourself to a new client, explain your background and credentials, make some marketing points about your business, and lay out the responsibilities that you expect the client to assume in the relationship.

Provider Information

This first section of your policies is where you provide general information about yourself and your approach to your child care business. Although I give this section the descriptive title "Provider Information," in your policies you may want to use a more informal name, such as "About Tinker Tots Child Care." This section could include any or all of the topics described below.

Your Child Care Philosophy

Your policy handbook offers the opportunity to share with your clients the goals of your business and your reasons for providing child care. You can do this with a short description of your views—for example, on child development or religion—and an explanation of how you will (or won't) share those views with the children.

This statement of your "provider philosophy" can help potential clients clearly understand what to expect from your child care program. It can also stimulate a discussion in which you can clarify your values further. Your philosophy statement isn't something that you would negotiate with your clients; it is a declaration of your beliefs. It can be short:

I run a child-centered program that focuses on the individual needs of each child.

This statement can also be quite lengthy, if you would like to explain your beliefs and values in more detail.

Your Mission Statement

Some providers create a more formal mission statement for their business. A mission statement is a brief (usually one-sentence) description of what your business aims to accomplish; it's purpose is to state the fundamental reason why you are in business. A formal mission statement will include the following elements:

- The name of your business
- What you intend to do
- How you intend to do it
- What the outcome will be

Here's an example of a mission statement for a family child care program:

Tinker Tots Child Care will provide licensed care for infants through school-age children in a loving, developmentally appropriate home environment that will allow each child to grow to his or her full potential.

Your Qualifications

This section gives you the opportunity to list the background and training you have that is relevant to caring for children. (Some providers organize this section like a resume, but you don't have to be that formal.) This might include your educational credentials, work experience, caregiving skills, professional affiliations, and any child care training and workshops that you have taken.

If you are accredited by the National Association for Family Child Care, or if you have a Child Development Associate Credential, be sure to highlight these accomplishments; they are objective signs of quality, and you should make sure that your clients are aware of them.

This is also a good place to provide your references—people your clients can call to ask about your work with children, such as some of your current or past clients. Be sure to get written permission from your references before you list their names (see page 99). If you are just starting out in business, you can list the names of friends, teachers, or clergy instead. If you have worked in another child care setting, you can list the name of your previous employer or supervisor.

Are You Licensed, Certified, or Registered?

If you are licensed, certified, or registered under your state laws, it's important to let your clients know. (If you aren't, you don't have to tell them, as long as you don't lie.) If you are, it is a mark of professionalism and tells clients that they are entitled to expect a higher quality of care than if you weren't.

In this section you can summarize the key aspects of your licensing rules (the number of children you are entitled to care for, your required qualifications and training, and so on) or you can explain how your clients can get a copy of the licensing rules that apply to you.

You should post a copy of your license, certificate, or registration where your clients can easily see it, and let them know how to contact your licensor if they have any questions or complaints about your program (see page 77).

Don't lie about having a license; if you do, it will invalidate your contract. This means that if your license is suspended or revoked, or if you are put on probation, you should inform your clients in writing of the change in your status. If you later try to enforce your contract and can't show that you informed the client that you had lost your license, a judge will most likely throw the case out of court on the grounds that you made a false (implied) claim about your program.

A change in your licensure status is also a liability issue; if you lose your license, your liability insurance will be invalidated—and your clients need to be informed of that change in your insurance coverage.

• •

Explain Your Role as a Mandated Reporter

In most states family child care providers are mandated reporters of child abuse or neglect. This means that you have a legal responsibility to keep children safe and to report any suspected neglect or abuse. In your policy handbook, you might want to tell your clients what you will do if a child has suspicious injuries or exhibits behavior that is symptomatic of neglect or abuse. (You may also want to tell your clients how they can report suspected abuse or neglect.) If you aren't sure what your legal responsibilities are, talk to your licensor or your local child protection office. If you are honest with your clients about your responsibility to report abuse, most of them will appreciate your efforts to keep their children safe.

• •

Your Liability Insurance

I strongly recommend that you carry adequate business liability insurance to protect both yourself and your clients. In some states the licensing laws require you to tell your clients whether you have business liability insurance or not—and if you don't have it, many states require you to get signed statements from your clients indicating that they understand this. Bear in mind that even if a client knows that you don't have liability insurance, she can still sue you if her child is injured. (For a comprehensive discussion of business liability insurance, see the *Legal and Insurance Guide*.)

Although I recommend that you carry business liability insurance and inform your clients about it, I don't recommend that you tell your clients the name of your insurance company or the amount of your coverage; they don't need to know this information.

Your Substitutes and Employees

There are situations in which you may need to have a substitute care for the children on a temporary basis; for example, when you have a doctor's appointment, training workshop, or family emergency, or if you take the children on a field trip. You may also have an employee who works with the children (especially if you are a group family child care provider and are required to have another adult with the children).

Since your clients have signed a contract with you to provide care for their child, you need to tell them before they sign your contract when you might use substitutes or employees. During the initial interview try to give the prospective client an idea of how often you might use a substitute. Clients don't usually object to this unless the use of substitutes is a regular occurrence.

If you have an employee who works with the children, your policies should explain her responsibilities, qualifications, and experience to reassure your clients that she is reliable and competent. This section should describe any training she has taken that will help protect the health and safety of the children. You may also wish to describe her role in your emergency plan (see page 86).

Your Privacy Policy

In times of growing identity theft, parents are increasingly concerned about their family's privacy; also, no one wants you to spread gossip about her family. You can reassure your clients by adopting a formal privacy policy that addresses these concerns. The policy should say that you'll keep all information about your clients and their children confidential unless you have written permission to share specific information. Here's a sample of such a policy:

> *I will do all that I can to protect your family's privacy and will abide by the state privacy law. I will keep all records and information about your child and your family private and confidential, unless I have your written permission to reveal specific information. I also ask you to respect the privacy of my family by not sharing any information about my family without my written permission.*

In your privacy policy you can include a privacy permission form in which you can specify all the ways that you'd like to share information about your clients and ask for their permission. For example, if you'd like to post photos of the children around your home or mention their names in your newsletter, you can ask your clients to give you permission to share this information. If a client objects to this, you can adjust the policy as needed to satisfy her concerns or make an exception for her child.

In your privacy policy you should also ask your clients to respect your privacy and that of your family. You may also want to set limits on when your clients may contact you. For example, you may need to specify that you aren't on call 24 hours a day. Otherwise, clients may feel free to call you at all hours, or a client may assume that it's okay to come over anytime to pick up clothing or personal items that her child has left behind, without calling in advance.

Your Nondiscrimination Clause

Discrimination—refusing to provide your services to clients who belong to certain groups or classes of people—is one of the few areas where your policies are regulated by law. Federal law prohibits you from discriminating against a client or child based on race, color, sex, disability, religion, or national origin. (Your state or locality may also outlaw discrimination based on marital status, sexual orientation, public assistance status, or other factors—check with your licensor or child care resource and referral agency for more information.)

You are bound by the discrimination laws whether you include them in your policies or not. However, you may still wish to include a statement in your policies that you don't discriminate, especially if you want to make it clear that you don't discriminate against certain groups that aren't protected by those laws, such as gay and lesbian families. (For more on how the discrimination laws affect family child care providers, see the *Legal and Insurance Guide*.)

The Rules of Your Home

In this section you might also want to list any rules of your home, such as asking clients and children to remove their shoes in your entryway or letting them know that the children in your care aren't allowed to sleep or play in certain areas of your home. For example, some providers keep their own children's bedrooms off-limits during business hours.

Client Responsibilities

In the next section of your policies you may want to detail your clients' responsibilities. By explaining the areas that you expect your clients to take responsibility for, you can improve communication, prevent misunderstandings, and explain what your clients need to do to keep the relationship running smoothly.

Encourage a Partnership with Your Clients

Caring for children is a cooperative partnership between you and your clients—to best meet their children's needs, your clients need to be actively involved in your program. Your policies can describe the ways that you will communicate with your clients and explain how you will expect them to participate in your program. For example, here are some activities that you might list:

- I will ask you to attend regular meetings to discuss your child's progress. (see page 14)
- I will give you a daily note that summarizes your child's day.
- I will ask you to fill out an evaluation of my program every year. (see page 15)

Since some people are more comfortable communicating in writing, while others prefer to communicate in person, try to give your clients the opportunity to share their thoughts in either way. However, when you have something negative to discuss about a child, it's best to sit down in person, rather than communicating through notes, e-mails, or voice mail. (Be sure to provide some positive feedback as well during the conversation.)

Updating Your Records for the Child

Your clients are responsible for providing you with information about the child and updating it as needed. For example, the licensing regulations in your state may require you to keep certain kinds of records for each child, such as emergency contact numbers, immunization records, and a list of the people who are authorized to pick up the child from your program. Even if these records aren't legally required, they may be necessary for emergency planning and can help to protect you in the event of a lawsuit.

For all these reasons, it's helpful to clearly list the specific documents or information that your clients must provide to you. You should review these records with your clients at least once a year to ensure that they are up-to-date.

Arranging Backup Care

Your policies should explain that there may be circumstances in which your clients will need a substitute caregiver—for example, if you get sick, go on vacation, or have a personal emergency. Although it may seem like a nice idea to help your clients by keeping a list of substitutes that you can call to arrange backup care, this isn't really your responsibility, and it may expose you to liability issues if the client doesn't get along with a backup caregiver.

Basically, you have four policy options in this area; you can make one of the following statements in your policies:

- *Clients must make their own arrangements for backup child care.*

- *It is the client's responsibility to arrange backup care, but the provider will suggest the names of some other caregivers to get them started. The provider cannot take responsibility for any problems that arise if the client uses one of the providers she has suggested.*

- *The provider will make an effort to call a few other caregivers in an attempt to arrange backup care for her clients. However, if the provider isn't able to find another caregiver, the clients will be responsible for finding a substitute.*

- *The provider will take on the responsibility of finding backup care for her clients.*

Although some providers take the last approach, I don't recommend it. This makes it hard to avoid liability issues—since you have arranged the substitute caregiver, a client may feel that you are responsible for any problems that arise with her. I suggest that you adopt one of the first two options listed above. (Another option is that it may be possible for your clients to take turns providing backup care for each other when you are not available.)

Whatever you decide, your policies should clearly explain what you are willing to do and what you expect your clients to do if you are temporarily unable to provide care. If you get involved in helping your clients find a substitute, make it clear that they are hiring the substitute directly, not through you, and state that you cannot take responsibility for any problems that arise with the substitute provider. This will at least help you to avoid liability if the client and the substitute don't get along.

Supplies Provided by the Client

It can be expensive to keep on hand all the supplies that the children in your care might need every day. One way to cut your costs is to ask your clients to provide some or all of certain supplies for their child. For example, this might include diapers (disposable or cloth), baby wipes, baby bottles, a pacifier, a nap blanket, sunscreen lotion, insect repellent, and so on. In your policies, you might also explain how you will label and store these items to satisfy your clients that the items they supply will be reserved for their child.

Dependent Care Plans

A growing number of employers offer dependent care plans (also called cafeteria plans or flexible benefit plans). Under these plans a client can set aside some of her pretax salary to pay for child care expenses. You should ask your clients if they participate in these plans; if they do, they are responsible for providing you with the appropriate forms and letting you know the rules and deadlines that you must follow to receive payment. The client's employer may provide the client with receipts that you must sign or the client may simply ask you to generate a receipt that she can submit to her employer.

You can also explain that if a client hasn't spent all the money that she has set aside by the end of the plan year, you will be asking her to give you the unspent money, since otherwise she will lose those funds, and you can use them to improve the quality of the child care that you provide for her.

Bad Weather Closings

There may be days when bad weather will require you to shut down your business. Bad weather may also shut down your clients' businesses or the schools that their children attend. When this happens, it will be helpful to have a policy statement that explains that you expect clients to notify you if their child will not be coming to your program, and that you will notify them if you decide to close your business for the day.

Your Grievance Procedure

In this section, encourage your clients to share any questions or concerns about your program and ask them to come to you as soon as possible whenever they have a problem or a complaint. You should be able to resolve most of the issues that your clients raise by communicating, listening, and negotiating a compromise if appropriate (see chapter 10).

However, you should also include your licensor's name and phone number in your policies—if a client isn't satisfied with your response, she should know how to contact your licensor. (If a client is unhappy and you don't seem to be able to resolve her complaint, contact your licensor right away to protect yourself against any false accusations.)

CHAPTER EIGHT

Caring for the Children

Chapter Summary
This chapter discusses the three policy topics that are directly related to
caring for the children—your program activities and policies; your safety,
health, and illness policies; and your policies for transporting the children.

The next section that you may wish to include in your policy handbook addresses all the
policies that relate to the child care that you provide. This would include a description of the
activities in your program, and your policies for disciplining children, handling illnesses, and
transporting the children.

Your Child Care Program

Children's Activities

The activities or curriculum that you provide for the children in your care are the heart of
your business. These activities can be highly structured, or they can be very informal. Since
children can learn in many different kinds of environments, it's helpful to start this section
with a statement that explains how the children will benefit from the activities that are
offered in your program.

After that, it's helpful to describe the activities that the children will participate in during
the day. However, it usually isn't helpful to specify an exact daily schedule for your program. If you say that you will do a certain activity during each part of the day, then your
clients will expect you to do so, and this will add unnecessary pressure if the children get
excited about some unscheduled activity. So if in your policies you would like to describe a
typical day, you might use the word "outline" rather than "schedule," to allow flexibility
in your program.

It's a good idea to review this description of the activities in your program with your current clients (and later with each potential new client). This opens the door for a good discussion about your philosophy of how children learn and what works well in your experience.
It also gives your clients a chance to tell you what they hope their children will learn in your
program.

For example, your policies might say, "I will conduct activities that challenge each child's creative talent and imagination." If one of your clients says that creativity and imagination are not as important as learning the skills that are necessary for success in school, this can be an opening for a discussion about how children learn when they use their imagination.

You may want to revise the description of the activities in your program after these discussions with your clients, to be sure that they reflect the points that you have discussed.

• •

Preschool Programs

Be clear what you mean when describing your program activities. For example, some family child care providers say that they offer a "preschool program"; however, many clients don't understand what this means. Technically, any provider who cares for preschool-aged children is offering a program for preschoolers. Usually the term "preschool program" means that the provider is conducting a more structured curriculum-based learning program for at least part of the day. She might offer child care in the morning and a more structured preschool program in the afternoon.

• •

Celebrating Birthdays and Holidays

Everybody loves a party, and your clients are likely to expect you to acknowledge birthdays and holidays in some way. Since these kinds of celebrations vary widely in family child care, it's helpful to explain your approach in your policies so that your clients will know what to expect. Some providers encourage the children in their care to bring presents when one of them has a birthday; others avoid an exchange of gifts in order to reduce the financial burden for their clients.

If you don't already have a celebration policy, you could poll your clients and ask them what days or events they would like your program to celebrate and how they would be willing to participate in those celebrations. This is an area where you may want to have some flexibility in order to meet the changing needs and expectations of your clients.

Clothing

Most family child care providers ask their clients to bring an extra set of clothing in case the child's clothes get soiled or wet during the day. This is another area that can be helpful to put in writing. For example, your policy might ask your clients to put an identifying mark on their clothes to help you identify the clothing for each child. You could also ask your clients to bring appropriate seasonal outdoor clothing in the winter and summer months.

Your policy might also describe how you will handle situations in which a child requires a change of clothes but his parent hasn't left any clothing with you. If you choose to use extra clothing that you happen to have on hand in this scenario, you may want to charge a fee for this service. (If you do, don't forget to spell out this fee in your contract.)

Food and Nutrition

Your policies can also explain what kind of food you will prepare for the children and when you will serve their meals. Since preparing and serving food can take a large part of your day, sharing your meal schedule may help your clients understand the consequences of arriving late. You can also post your menus on a bulletin board or make them available upon request. If you encourage your clients to visit your program during the day, let them know whether they are welcome during mealtimes and how they might be able to help you if they are.

Other policy issues related to food and nutrition include special diets and infant feeding. Ask your new clients whether their children have any food allergies and explain how you will handle special dietary requests. With the parents of infants and young children, discuss when and how to wean the child from a bottle to a cup or from a formula to solid food, and whether it is acceptable to give the child a pacifier. You will need continuing communication with the parents to make these kinds of transitions run smoothly.

Naps and Quiet Time

If you have to manage your daily schedule to meet the needs of several children, it may not be possible for you to be flexible and allow some children to follow a different schedule. If so, it's helpful to explain this in your policies. Otherwise a client may ask you to give her child a longer or shorter nap, or no nap at all. It will be easier to insist on following your usual schedule if you cover this topic in your policies.

In this section you may also wish to describe what you are doing to protect infants from Sudden Infant Death Syndrome (SIDS), such as making sure that infants are always laid down to sleep on their back.

Helping Children Learn to Use the Toilet

It is perfectly legal to have a policy that you won't care for children who haven't yet learned to use the toilet. However, you can't agree to care for some children who aren't toilet-trained but then exclude others because they have special needs. For example, some providers set a specific age by which the children in their care must successfully use the toilet in order to continue in their program; however, you may not be able to enforce that age for a child who has special needs, since this is likely to be considered a "reasonable accommodation" under the Americans with Disabilities Act (ADA) guidelines.

If you accept the responsibility of helping children learn to use the toilet, your policies should describe the methods that you will use. Will you use pull-ups? Will you use rewards? Will you teach boys to sit or to stand at the toilet? (Be sure to ask the client to supply lots of underwear and pull-up pants.)

When you are helping a child learn to use the toilet, it is imperative that you and the client agree on a plan—and your policies can be the first step in this direction. If a child is having difficulty, you may want to ask the parents for additional help, such as taking time off work to come to your program and assist you.

Some providers charge more if a child isn't toilet-trained. If you are considering this option, bear in mind that it may lead to problems, since it encourages clients to pressure their children to use the toilet in order to reduce the cost of child care.

Toys

Some family child care providers have a policy that children are not allowed to bring their own toys into the provider's home. Personal toys can create conflicts between children, especially if another child damages or breaks a toy. You may also wish to limit toys from home if you are concerned that they won't be developmentally appropriate for the other children in your care. Some providers also forbid any type of toy weapon, such as toy guns or swords, because they encourage battle play, and someone may get hurt.

You may also wish to limit the number of personal toys that a child may have in your home at a time. Some providers allow each child to have one special stuffed animal or blanket that is only brought out at naptime.

If you do allow children to bring their own toys from home, it shouldn't be your responsibility to replace a toy that is broken by another child, and you may want to address this in your policies. If a child loses a toy during the day, you shouldn't have to spend a lot of time looking for it at the end of the day. Tell the child (and her parent) that you will look for it the next day.

You should also consider whether you will allow the children in your care to play with your own children's toys. Although there is no right or wrong about this issue, do ask your own children how they feel about it. The easiest answer might be to just put these toys away during business hours.

Behavior Guidance

Your policies for handling behavior problems require an especially high level of communication with your clients. Parents have widely different approaches to disciplining their children, and each client will expect you to follow her lead. (However, your first responsibility is to follow your state's laws, regardless of what the client wants; see below.) See the worksheets on the CD for examples of the language you might use in your policies.

The best time to raise the topic of behavior guidance is the initial interview with a potential client, since your clients should understand up front what to expect from you. One way to bring this up is to ask the client how she would handle the following situations:

- Her child bites another child.
- Her child threatens another child.
- Her child refuses to share a toy with another child.
- Her child pulls down his pants in front of another child.

Listen to her replies, and then explain how you would handle these situations and how you would expect her to support your actions. In this discussion, use "what if" scenarios such as those given above to help clarify each other's expectations.

Corporal Punishment

What should you do if a client says that she wants you to spank her child if he misbehaves? First, contact your licensing worker or local child protection agency to find out whether corporal punishment (spanking) is allowed in your state. If your state law forbids corporal punishment, you must obey the law, regardless of whether you or the child's parent believes it is right. If you violate state law, you can lose your license, even if you are following the client's instructions.

If your state does allow corporal punishment, you can still have a policy that it won't be used in your home. What goes on in your business is up to you. If you feel uncomfortable with the way a client asks you to discipline her child, listen to your instincts; you can simply tell her that you aren't comfortable with handling the situation that way.

Even if it's allowed in your state, spanking the children in your care can lead to big problems and poses significant legal risks—and as a result I recommend that you never or rarely spank a child. Even if the client has given you permission, if she later gets angry at you for any reason, she may decide to accuse you of child abuse.

If you still wish to have the option of spanking the children in your care, you need to get written permission from the child's parents first. If the parents are married or living together, be sure to get the signatures of both parents. Keep a record of each time you spank a child and report it to the client at the end of the day so that she remains fully informed of your actions.

Whatever you decide, it will be helpful to spell out your rules about corporal punishment in your policies. See the worksheets on the CD for examples of the language you could use in your policies.

• •

Q & A: Behavior Problem

Q: One of the children in my care has developed a behavior problem that I can't seem to resolve. The parents and I have tried to work out ways to deal with it, but nothing seems to work. The child's behavior is seriously disrupting the other children. What should I do?

A: If you and your client have run out of ideas, seek outside help. You may want to talk to the child's doctor or an expert in child development. Also ask your local child care resource and referral agency for help. If the child has a disability, you must make a "reasonable effort" to provide care for the child. If the child doesn't have a disability and you can't prevent him from seriously disrupting the other children, you could ask the client to keep the child away from your home for a week or two to see if he calms down. If nothing works, your last resort is to terminate your contract with the client; the child may do better in a different child care home.

• •

Your Illness, Health, and Safety Policies

Your policies about illnesses, injuries, and medical care are especially important, since they deal with the health of the children and raise issues that can involve significant risks for your business. (For a discussion of the legal risks, see the *Legal and Insurance Guide*.)

The first decision in your illness policy is whether you will care for children who are sick. Your state licensing rules may not allow you to care for seriously ill children; however, even if this is allowed, you should exercise caution in caring for children who are very sick or who have a serious contagious illness, to protect the other children and your business.

If you are willing to care for children who are ill, you should clarify what your limits are. In most states it is up to you whether to care for mildly ill children, and it is always acceptable to have a policy that you won't provide care for even mildly ill children. Most family child care providers have an illness notification policy that spells out exactly when clients should keep their ill children at home. Here's an example:

Children with the following kinds of illnesses may not attend my program: a contagious disease, a virus, an illness that includes vomiting, a temperature over 100 degrees, pink eye, a rash, diarrhea, parasitic infection, or other illnesses such as _____. If your child has any of these symptoms, you are required to notify me as soon as possible. The child won't be allowed to return to my program until he or she has been symptom-free for a full 24 hours.

• •

Sudden Infant Death Syndrome

Sudden Infant Death Syndrome (SIDS) poses a serious health risk for infants. You should educate yourself about SIDS and make it a policy to always put infants to sleep on their backs. (To find out more about SIDS, visit www.sidscenter.org or see the *Legal and Insurance Guide*.) If a client asks you to put her baby to sleep on his stomach, you should proceed as follows before you agree:

• Ask your licensor whether you legally can (or should) comply with this request.
• Ask for a written confirmation from the child's doctor that the child must sleep on his stomach because of a medical condition.
• Get written permission from the client.

However, even with permission from the licensor, doctor, and client, many providers won't allow an infant to sleep on his stomach because of the liability risk involved.

If a client drops off a sleeping infant in a car seat, be sure to check that the baby is breathing normally before the client leaves. There have been cases where a child was dropped off in a car seat, apparently fast asleep, and the provider later discovered that the child had actually died of SIDS.

• •

Administering Medication

Before you write your policies about dispensing medications to children, find out if there are any state laws that you have to follow and whether you are allowed to do so. Even if your state allows you to give medication to the children, you can always choose not to do so, to protect yourself from legal liability if something goes wrong. (If a child has a disability, check with your licensor to find out whether you are required to administer her medication.) If you do administer medication to the children in your care, always follow explicit directions from the client or the child's doctor. Here's an example of a medication policy:

> *You must sign a separate written authorization for each prescription that you would like me to dispense to your child. The medicine must be in its original container, labeled with the child's name and the instructions for administering it. (You should ask the pharmacist to split each prescription into two containers, one for me and one for you, each with a full label and instructions.)*

If the medication hasn't been prescribed by a doctor, you should still get written authorization from the client before you administer it. If you have any questions about whether a child is getting the proper medical treatment, contact your licensor.

Another good policy is to require your clients to notify you if they have given a child any medication at home within the previous 24 hours.

Current Immunizations Are Required

Most states have laws that require parents to have their children immunized, and you may be required to keep records showing that the immunizations of each child in your program are up-to-date. If one of your clients objects to the requirement that her child be immunized, you can refuse to provide care for the child. However, if the parent's objection is based on religious grounds, you should contact your licensor for advice before terminating care, to ensure that you don't run afoul of the laws against religious discrimination.

Smoking and Drinking

Many state licensing laws prohibit smoking in any family child care home. But even if you aren't bound by this prohibition, bear in mind that secondhand smoke poses real health hazards to children, and it's important to take steps to reduce their exposure to secondhand smoke as much as possible.

A woman once called our office to complain that her family child care provider refused to let her smoke in the day care home, and she thought this was a case of illegal discrimination. We responded that although it was discrimination, it wasn't against the law. In fact, the laws in her state (as in many states) prohibit clients from smoking in a family child care home.

Some states also require family child care providers to have a policy about drinking and drugs. This can be a simple matter of stating that you do not drink or do drugs, and your clients must follow the same rules while in your home. Another option would be to state that you and your employees do not drink or do drugs during business hours.

Emergency Policy

Your policies should explain to your clients how your program is prepared for emergencies and how you (and your employees) will respond in the event of an emergency. Your plan might explain what you are doing to reduce the risk of fires or accidents and what you teach the children to do in an emergency situation. For example, you might say:

- *To reduce the risk of fire, I follow the fire safety rules and state laws regarding smoke detectors and fire extinguishers.*

- *I teach the children that if there is ever a fire in the house, they should run out of the house and meet in the backyard.*

- *In case the power goes out, I keep a first aid kit, flashlights, and extra blankets on each floor.*

- *I teach the children about household safety and personal safety when we leave my home.*

- *I keep near my phone a list of emergency phone numbers (police, hospital, ambulance) and the contact numbers for all my clients.*

- *I bring these contact numbers with me whenever I take the children on a field trip or other excursion away from home.*

• •

The Importance of Emergency Contact Information

In your policies, emphasize the importance of being able to reach your clients in an emergency. At one program a child was stung four times by a bee and had a serious allergic reaction. After getting immediate medical help, the provider tried to contact the parents, but found that their pagers and cell phones were all turned off. To avoid this problem, ask your clients to regularly check for messages on their pager, voice mail, or cell phone. Also ask them to notify you if they leave work early, temporarily change their work location, or otherwise vary their normal routine.

• •

When a Child Is Injured in Your Care

This section of your policies should also explain how you will handle a child who becomes injured in your care. If you are required to take first aid or CPR classes, you may wish to state that here, so that your clients will know that you are trained to handle common injuries and accidents.

In most states you are required to follow certain reporting procedures when a child is injured in your program. Your injury policy may include a requirement that the client pick up the injured child as soon as possible. However, when an injury occurs, I suggest that you first address the child's immediate needs (if the injury is serious, call 911 right away), and then contact the parent as soon as possible after that.

● ●

Document Injuries When the Children Arrive

You may want to make a quick note of each child's physical condition as the children arrive at your program and when they are picked up at the end of the day. If you notice that a child seems to have any medical symptoms or physical injuries, you could ask the parent to sign a statement that the child arrived in that condition. This policy can help protect you against false claims of child abuse.

● ●

When a Child Becomes Ill in Your Care

Your illness policy should address how you will handle a child who becomes ill in your care. I suggest that you first address the child's immediate needs, if necessary by calling 911, and then contact the child's parent. (For more advice about how to handle children who become ill, contact your local child care resource and referral agency.) You may wish to have a policy that the client must pick up the child as soon as possible.

Your illness policy should also explain that you will notify your clients if the children are exposed to an illness while in your program. If you discover that a child's illness presents a threat to the other children in your program, you should contact all your other clients immediately and explain the illness that the other children have been exposed to.

Pets

There are many kinds of household pets that can be a valuable learning experience for the children in your care, such as fish, parakeets, gerbils, mice, and ants in a farm. However, dogs and cats can pose some special problems. No matter how gentle your pet is with your family, it may be a danger to other people and children. For this reason, some state licensing laws restrict dogs and cats from being in contact with the children in family child care.

If you have a dog or a cat in your home, it's important to inform your clients about this in your policies and explain how you will ensure the safety of their children. You should have business liability insurance that will protect you if your pet injures a child. However, many insurance companies won't insure you if there is a dog in your home.

Water Hazards

Wading pools, swimming pools, rivers, and lakes are all water hazards that pose a serious risk of drowning for young children. If there are any water hazards on your property or near your home, you should talk to your liability insurance company about this to make sure that you would be covered in the event of an accident. Your insurance company may require you to take specific steps to provide that coverage—for example, if your property borders on a lake or river, you may need to fence off the waterfront access. In your policies, inform your clients about the water hazard and the steps you are taking to keep the children safe.

Swimming pools are also dangerous to children. If there is a swimming pool on your property, your policies should inform your clients and explain how you are keeping the children in your care safe. Follow any state laws about fencing your pool or your property and always get written permission before you let a child use a pool.

Your Policies for Transporting Children

The various ways that you or your clients may transport the children before, during, and after your program can raise complex issues and pose significant risks to your business that could involve liability insurance, vehicle insurance, and your role as a mandated reporter. The topics that you should address in your policies include whether you will transport the children in your own car, how you will handle field trips, who is authorized to pick up and drop off the child, and how school-age children may be transported to and from your program. (See the *Legal and Insurance Guide* for more information about these topics.)

Transporting Children in Your Car

It's becoming more common for family child care providers to make it a policy not to transport the children they care for in their own vehicle. The reasons for this trend are the high cost of car insurance and the fact that many car insurance companies are increasingly either unwilling to insure family child care providers when they transport the children or—if they are willing to do so—now require the provider to buy very expensive commercial vehicle insurance.

If you do wish to transport the children in your own vehicle, you should take the following steps before you begin doing so:

- Get written permission from your clients to transport the children in your car.
- Make sure that you are using car seats or seat belts as required by your state's laws.
- Make sure that your car insurance policy will cover any accidents that occur while you are using the car for business purposes.

If someone else will be helping you transport the children in another vehicle, then you will also need to get written permission to have the children transported by that person, even if the other driver is one of your clients.

Field Trips

Your field trip policy gives you an opportunity to describe the learning activities that the children in your care will experience away from your home. However, since trips away from your home also raise safety concerns, your field trip policy should explain the safety precautions that you will take on all your field trips; for example:

> *On every field trip I carry a first aid kit and the emergency contact numbers for all the parents. I also have a field trip emergency plan.*

If you or anyone else will be transporting the children by car, you will need to take the safety precautions described in the previous section.

You should also get specific written permission before you take the children on any field trip. The Forms folder on the CD includes a field trip permission form. You could ask your clients to sign a general field trip permission form when they enroll, and then ask them to sign a specific permission form for each trip (also see the *Legal and Insurance Guide*).

Who Is Authorized to Pick Up and Drop Off the Child?

Your policies should also explain your rules about who is authorized to pick up a child from your care. To avoid legal trouble, you should have a strict policy that you will release a child only to your client or to another person whom the client has authorized in writing to pick up the child. Your policies might ask each client to identify at least two other people who are authorized to pick up the child. Get photos of the authorized persons, and if possible arrange to meet them, so that you will be sure to recognize them when they show up at your door.

• •

If Anyone Else Tries to Claim a Child

If anyone who is not on the authorized list shows up to claim a child, take all reasonable steps to try to stop the person from taking the child. Don't open your front door to a stranger. Ask the person to leave. Threaten to call the police if the person doesn't leave immediately. However, you should not try to physically prevent the person from taking the child. If the person does take the child, write down the car license number, and immediately call 911. Then notify the client.

• •

Biological Parents and Custody Disputes

Another area that you may wish to explain in your policies is the issue of biological parents and custody disputes. You are always required to release a child to a biological parent unless a court has taken away that parent's custodial rights. In other words, one parent cannot prevent another parent from picking up their child from your care. Unfortunately, this means that family child care providers are increasingly being caught in the middle of custody disputes.

For example, one day a client says to you, "My husband and I are in the process of getting a divorce. I'm afraid that he might take Elise and flee to another state. I don't want you to let him pick her up anymore." What should you do? What is your responsibility?

A child's biological parents are always entitled to custody of the child (including the right to pick her up from your care at any time), unless a court order has limited those rights. For this reason, you should always assume that both biological parents have full custody rights, even if one of them hasn't been authorized by the other parent to pick up the child. However, if a client gives you a copy of a court order or divorce decree that limits the other parent's rights, then you must follow that document. For example, if the court order says that the father may only have custody of the child on Mondays and Wednesdays, then you must only allow him to pick up the child on those two days.

So how should you respond to the mother who has asked you not to let the father pick up the child? Your would have to answer,

> *I'm sorry, but I can't do that. The law says that both parents have the right to pick up the child, and I can't prevent him from picking her up unless you can give me a court order that limits his custody rights. If you have such a court order, I will be happy to follow its directions.*

Make sure that the mother understands that it is her responsibility to get a court order and give it to you before you can act. Read the court order and use your best judgment about what it means. If you aren't sure what it means, ask the mother to explain it to you. If the father disputes her interpretation and says that it means something else, then inform him that he will need to have a lawyer or judge clarify it for you.

Pickup and Drop-off Policy

You should have a pickup policy that explains your role in ensuring the safety of the children when your clients drop them off or pick them up. If a client arrives or departs with a child and you can see that he is intoxicated or isn't using a proper car seat for the child, you are faced with two potential risks:

- In most states you are legally mandated to report child neglect or abuse. Failing to report that you saw a child in a dangerous situation (with a drunken driver or without a proper car seat) could put you in violation of this law and cause you to lose your child care license.

- If the child is injured in a car accident after leaving your home, the parents could sue you because you were aware of the danger to the child and did nothing to prevent it—and they might even win. In this situation, a court might hold you partly liable for the accident.

However, if you didn't have any reason to believe that the driver was incapacitated or if you weren't able to see that the child wasn't placed in a car seat (because you were in another room and couldn't see the car) then you are unlikely to be held liable.

Your pickup policy should state that since your primary concern is the safety of the children in your care, you will not tolerate a client who fails to use an appropriate car seat or who transports a child while in an incapacitated state. If you see this happening, you will take steps to keep the child safe. This might include asking the client for the name of someone else who could pick up the child, calling a cab, or some other alternative. If a client refuses to follow your policy and insists on taking the child anyway, you should call 911. (It's a good idea to record the license number of all the cars your clients use to pick up their children so that you will have the number readily available in this situation.)

If you have such a policy, make sure that your clients understand your expectations. Ask them to sign the policy, to reinforce how serious it is. If a client refuses to cooperate with this policy, you should end her contract. If a client has trouble remembering to bring a proper car seat, you might suggest that he purchase an extra car seat and leave it with you, so that he can use it when he arrives without one. Don't loan a client a car seat that you own. If there is an accident and the seat is found to be defective, he may sue you.

If a client drops off a child at your program while in an intoxicated state or without an appropriate car seat or carrier, it won't do any good to call the police, because the child is no longer in the car. Instead, warn the client that you will not tolerate this behavior, and if it happens again, it will be grounds for immediately terminating care.

If a client objects to your pickup or drop-off policy, saying that it is none of your business whether he uses a proper car seat when driving to or from your home, respond tactfully by saying that the child's safety is your primary concern and that you don't want any unnecessary injuries to occur. (If he pushes you further, you could remind him that you are a mandated reporter.) However, most of your clients are likely to be grateful that you are showing so much concern for the safety of their children.

• •

Don't Ask Your Clients to Sign a Liability Waiver

Some providers try to deal with pickup and drop-off issues by asking their clients to sign a liability waiver such as the following:

> *Client agrees not to hold the provider responsible for any injuries suffered while the child is in the client's car, such as before drop-off and after pickup each day.*

Other policies might include similar language for field trips or include a general liability waiver for any accident that occurs while the child is in their home. However, all of these kinds of liability waivers are worthless and won't be enforced by a court; your clients can't give up their right to sue you. (Even the children in your care can sue you years later.) The best way to protect yourself from liability risks is to buy adequate business liability insurance and adopt a pickup policy that is similar to the one in Sample Policy 3 in Appendix A. (Also see the box on page 30.)

• •

Transporting School-age Children

There are additional issues that may arise once children reach school age and require transportation to and from school or are allowed to travel on their own. A client may ask whether you are willing to pick up or drop off a child at school or at the bus stop every day. Another client may inform you that she is arranging for her child to walk or bike home or to a bus stop after your program. Still another client may ask if you would be willing to pick up his child at school if she becomes ill during the day. Before you agree to any of these arrangements, you should take the following steps:

- Check with your licensor to make sure that the proposed arrangement wouldn't violate any of the state licensing laws that regulate your supervision of children.
- Contact a local child protection agency and ask if the proposed arrangement would be considered dangerous to the child and trigger your role as a mandated reporter.
- Call your business liability insurance agent to find out if your policy would cover you if the child was injured during this time.
- If all of the above points check out, ask yourself if you really feel comfortable with the proposed arrangement. If you aren't comfortable, don't agree to it. It's better to go with your instincts than to consent to something that will bother you.
- If you feel comfortable with the arrangement and you wish to agree to it, you still need to get written permission from both parents first, even if it's their idea in the first place.

It can be helpful to spell out your policy about transporting school-age children before and after your program. Here are some examples of how you could phrase this:

- *I will not pick up a child from school due to illness.*

- *I am willing to take responsibility for accompanying a child to and from the nearest bus stop each day.*

- *Children will not be allowed to leave my program on their own; they must be picked up by a parent or other authorized person.*

PART IV

Making Your Contract and Policies Work

CHAPTER NINE

Before You Sign the Contract

Chapter Summary
This chapter explains the steps that you should take before a new client
signs your contract, to establish a good foundation for the relationship and
to reduce the likelihood of future problems.

After you write your contract and policies, you still need to implement and enforce them
effectively. In this part of the book I will discuss how to make those documents work for
you. This chapter will deal with the first part of that process—including some steps that you
should take long before the client ever sees your contract and policies.

When you meet a new client, getting her to sign your contract shouldn't be your first con-
sideration. There are seven steps that you should take to reduce the likelihood of future problems *before* you enroll a child in your program—and signing your contract will usually be
the final step in this process. These seven steps are:

1. Assess the initial contact
2. Conduct a client interview
3. Review your contract and policies
4. Check the client's references
5. Decide whether to enroll the child
6. Complete a trial period
7. Sign the contract

You may not need to follow all of the above steps in every case, and you can do the steps
before signing the contract in a different order; however, I will use this seven-step process as
a model to illustrate the kinds of issues that you should consider before you enter a contractual relationship with a new client.

You'll be able to do some of these steps relatively quickly, while others will take more
time. The important thing is not to feel rushed into enrolling any new client; taking the time
to carefully assess a potential client and her child is one of the best ways to prevent problems later on.

● ●

Consult the Family Child Care Marketing Guide

The *Family Child Care Marketing Guide* is an invaluable resource for the seven steps discussed in this chapter. Among other things, this book explains how to pro-mote your program, how to talk about your rates, how to identify the client's needs, how to listen to a client, how to conduct an interview, and how to do a tour of your home. The book also contains a Client Interview Checklist, a Choosing Child Care Checklist for clients, and an Enrollment Form.

● ●

Assess the Initial Contact

Typically a new client will contact you by phone and start by asking you some questions about your program. During this conversation, you have two goals—you're trying to both make a good first impression and screen out anyone who is obviously unsuitable for your program. In this initial contact, you will briefly describe the benefits of your program and attempt to answer the following questions:

- What are the specific needs of this parent and child?
- Does the family seem to be a match for my program?

If it sounds as if the family might be a good fit for your program, you would go to the next step by asking the client to come to your home for an interview.

Conduct an Interview

The purpose of the interview is to find out more about the family to help you determine whether they will be a good fit for your program. It also provides another opportunity for you to promote the benefits of your program.

At the beginning of the interview, make it clear that enrolling the child in your program will have to be a mutual decision. In other words, some clients assume that the choice to participate in your program is up to them, and that your role is just to go along with whatev-er they decide. To avoid this kind of misunderstanding, tell the client from the start that "to enroll your child, we will both need to agree that it is the right decision."

When you schedule the interview, tell the client how long the meeting will take—you will need enough time to conduct a tour of your home, go over all the details of how you operate your business, and allow plenty of time for both parties to ask and answer questions.

Tour Your Home

During the interview, show the client the places where the children in your care play, eat, and nap. Point out any special toys, equipment, or other special features of your home. Also point out all the precautions you have taken to keep the children safe, such as outlet covers, gates, fences, and locked storage of hazardous materials.

If the interview takes place during your program day, introduce the prospective client (and her child, if present) to your family and to the other children in your care. Describe your family's routine and activities and how they affect the children in your program. For example, if you must begin cooking dinner for your family by 6 PM or if you must drive your daughter to band practice at 5:30, you should explain this so that the client understands why your 5:15 pickup deadline isn't negotiable.

Describe Your Program

In the next part of the interview, describe your program. For example, you might wish to review your contract and policies at this point, as described in the next step. If you prefer, you can do this in a separate meeting; the important thing is to take the time to carefully review those documents before a new client signs your contract.

If you are licensed (or certified), show the prospective client your license. Discuss what your license does and doesn't cover in regard to the children's safety, health, and daily activities. If you have an employee who sometimes works with the children, introduce her (if possible) and explain her responsibilities.

Most family child care providers also ask a substitute to care for the children on a temporary basis when they have a doctor's appointment or a family emergency. Explain whom you will call on as a substitute and under what circumstances. Tell the prospective client how often you have used a substitute in the past year, to reassure her that this won't be more than an occasional occurrence.

Question and Answer Time

During the question and answer time, use open-ended questions to help you better understand whether the client's needs are a good match with yours. An open-ended question is one that can't be answered by yes or no, such as:

- *What's the most important thing I could do to help your child grow?*

- *What are your child's special interests?*

- *What do you see your child doing in three months, one year, or five years?*

During the interview take notes of the client's answers. Does the client seem willing to be flexible and adapt to your rules? Are there any signs that the child may be difficult to care for? Did the client raise any questions that concerned you? What are the likely advantages and disadvantages of enrolling this family?

Warning Signs

While you are getting to know the client during the interview, be alert for the following warning signs, which may indicate that it wouldn't be a good idea to enroll this child:

- Was the client unreasonably late for the interview? If so, this may be suggestive of things to come.

- Did the client show an interest in how you will care for their child? If not, you may later become frustrated trying to involve her in addressing the child's needs.
- Does the client seem to share your values? If not, can you both be respectful of each other's views and be comfortable talking about them? A client who has trouble handling conflict may later decide just to leave rather than work out a problem.
- Perhaps the most important area of potential conflict is how the client disciplines the child at home. If you differ significantly on this topic, it is a sign that the family may not be a good match for your program.
- During the interview, let the child play with the other children in your care and observe her behavior. For example, if the new child climbs all over the furniture, does this bother you? Does the client object to your telling the child not to climb on the furniture? Some habits may be hard to break.
- Finally, does the client treat you with respect and have a positive attitude about your ability to care for children? It's best to avoid self-centered people who are inconsiderate of you and your profession.

As you listen and observe, notice your gut feelings about the prospective client and her child. If one or both of them seems difficult to handle during the interview, the chances are that things won't get any easier later. Also, if a client doesn't seem to respect the policies and expectations that are required to run your business in a professional way, it's probably best not to enter into a working relationship with her.

Some providers take the extra step of doing a background check on their prospective clients. If you wish to do this, you can start by finding out if your county or state Web site allows you to search by name for convictions in criminal or civil court, traffic violations, and fines.

Review Your Contract and Policies

Either during the initial interview or later, set aside enough time to review your contract and policies. Since many family child care providers are uncomfortable discussing business, it may be tempting to just push some papers into a prospective client's hands and say,

> *Here's my contract; you'll need to sign it. My policies are attached, and you can read them later when you have the time.*

However, a professional provider will take the time to make sure that the prospective client understands all her contract terms and policies and will address any concerns. This can prevent misunderstandings before they occur and will make it much easier to enforce your rules and to resolve any conflicts that do arise later.

In the discussion, point out the most important points of your contract, such as your hours of operation, rates, and late fees. Occasionally stop to ask the prospective client if she has any questions about what you are saying. Also bear in mind that some people will need some time to absorb all the details of a long written agreement.

You may want to ask the prospective client to read a particular contract term or policy and explain what it means in her own words. When you do so, you may discover that her understanding is very different from yours. When this happens, ask her how you might clarify the meaning of that passage, and then adjust the wording until you find that your prospective clients can clearly understand what it means.

In reviewing your policies, describe your philosophy of caring for children and discuss how you will handle key issues, such as behavior guidance, naps, or helping children learn to use the toilet. Then ask the client about her parenting philosophy. How does her approach to raising children differ from yours? Ask her what she thinks of your contract and policies. Has she used other family child care providers before, and if so, what kinds of problems arose in this relationship?

Use the interview as an opportunity to sell yourself by pointing out your strengths, such as your years of experience, educational background, special training or equipment, varied activity schedule, comfortable indoor and outdoor play areas, and so on. Also be sure to describe your expectations of your clients. If the client doesn't feel comfortable with some of the terms in your contract or if she says that she needs more time to review your agreement, allow her to take it home, but don't sign it before you give it to her (see page 40).

Check the Client's References

The Client Will Ask for Your References

Prospective clients are likely to ask you for references before they decide to enroll their child. They do this because they want to learn more about you—are you a reliable, responsible, and caring person? This is a reasonable request, and you should have a list of several names available to give them.

The best kinds of references are current or former clients who have had a child in your care for many years. When a good client leaves your program, ask him if he would be willing to give you a reference for prospective clients. If he says yes, get written permission to use his name by having him sign a brief permission form:

I give _____ [your name] *permission to give my name and phone number to potential clients as a reference.*

Make sure to have the client sign and date this permission form. (You can use the sample provided in the Forms section of the CD.)

Ask the Client to Give You Her References

Although it may seem awkward, I recommend that you also ask potential clients to give you at least one or two child care references, including the names of their previous caregivers. You are about to make an important decision whether to spend every day with the child and enter into a contractual agreement with the parents. So it isn't unreasonable to want to know more about the family.

You can ask the parent to sign a simple permission form to allow the previous caregiver to answer your questions:

I, _____ [name of parent], *give permission for* _____ [name of previous caregiver] *to answer questions from* _____ [your name] *regarding the care s/he gave to my child from* _____ *to* _____ [dates of care].

If a client refuses to give you a reference, ask why, and use your own judgment to determine whether her answer is plausible. There are two circumstances in which you can't reasonably expect to get a reference for a previous provider—if the child has never been in child care before (for example, in the case of an infant), or if the client hasn't yet told her current provider that she is thinking of leaving. However, with the exception of these two circumstances, I don't recommend that you enroll a client who refuses to give you any child care references.

• •

If You Are Asked to Provide a Reference

If another child care provider asks you to provide a reference for a former client, you need to (1) respect the client's privacy and (2) avoid saying anything that could lead you to being accused of slander.

Before you say anything—in fact, before you even confirm that the person was a client—you need to have his written permission. Tell the provider who is asking for the reference that it's your policy not to share any information without permission, and that you will call her back after she sends you that permission.

What if you have something negative to say about the former client? If you make a statement that damages his reputation in the community, you will have committed slander, and he will have the right to sue you for damages. You will have a solid legal defense if you can prove that the statement is true. Your legal defense will be weak if the statement is too vague to be proved, such as "He always paid me late."

This means you should avoid sharing your interpretations and opinions and limit your statements to facts that you can prove. For example, you might say, "His payment was late seven times in four months," if you have the records to support that claim.

Although a former client is unlikely to actually sue you for slander, making broad allegations about your previous clients is unprofessional and can only create unnecessary trouble. For more information about slander and giving references, see chapter 12 of the *Legal and Insurance Guide*.

• •

Once the prospective client has given you the names of at least one or two child care references, call them and ask the following five questions:

1. How long did you care for the child?
2. Did you have any problems with the child or the parents that I should know about?
3. What are some positive things that you can tell me about this child and the parents?
4. If you had the opportunity, would you provide care for this child again?
5. Do you have any suggestions that may help the child make the transition to my program?

The fourth question is probably the most important one, so listen carefully to that answer. Bear in mind that you are looking for any *major* problems that might affect your relationship with the child or the client. Don't worry about minor issues, such as the client picking up the child late once or twice a year or the child occasionally crying for an hour after the client leaves. Major problems might include leaving the program without paying the provider in full or the child continually getting sick because her parents wouldn't take her to a doctor.

As you listen, also consider that different people will respond differently to conflict. The issues that upset the previous provider may not bother you, and vice versa. In addition, you should treat everything you are told with discretion. If the other provider makes an allegation about her previous client (such as "The father smokes marijuana"), you may be guilty of slander if you repeat it to anyone else (see below).

Decide Whether to Enroll the Child

After you have checked the prospective client's child care references you will be ready to make a decision about whether to enroll the child. That decision may be an easy one—you might be looking forward to caring for the child—or it may be more difficult. If you aren't sure what to do, take the time you need to think it over.

You should never feel obligated to care for a child just because the parents have asked you to. So many providers who talk to me about a conflict with a client have said, "I knew that this person was trouble right from the start. I could tell that we were going to have problems." If you feel uneasy about a client at this point, don't be afraid to turn her down. If you know that the relationship won't last, consider the child's best interests—resist the urge to care for him if you know he will only have to change providers again in a short time.

It can be hard to turn down a potential client. However, your decision should ultimately be based on what is best for the child and the other children in your care. It's better to say no than to enroll the child and have to terminate care six months later because of a conflict that you anticipated from the start.

Turning Down a Client

If you decide not to enroll a child, inform the parents in neutral language that doesn't blame them or their child. Don't say anything negative, such as "I don't trust that you will pay me on time," or "I don't think your child will be accepted by the other children in my program." These kinds of statements will only offend the parents unnecessarily—and a person who feels ill-treated is more likely to bad-mouth you or your program to other prospective clients.

The best way to turn down a parent is to simply say, "I don't think that my program is the best place for your child at this time" or "Unfortunately my program cannot meet your expectations." If she asks you for more specific reasons, don't elaborate. If you feel that you must say more, you can add, "It's not personal. I try to make the decision based on what's best for your child, and I have the feeling that he would be better off in someone else's care." The parents can't argue with your intuitions.

In turning down a potential client, some providers try to avoid hurt feelings by saying something like:

> *I'm waiting to hear from another prospective client who I interviewed last week. If she decides to enroll with me, I won't have a spot for your child. If I don't hear from her by Friday, I'll give you a call.*

Although it may be tempting to make up this kind of story, it can also get you into trouble. Let's say that you use this approach to get rid of a potential client, and the next week she sees that you are still running a newspaper ad and posting your flyers at the grocery store— or that she hears through the grapevine that you enrolled another child in your program after turning her down. She may accurately conclude that you weren't honest with her, and feel insulted. At this point she could complain to your licensor or even decide that you must have discriminated against her and submit a complaint to the human rights department. For these reasons, I recommend that you inform parents in a straightforward way that you have chosen not to enroll their child.

• •

Discrimination

Although you don't need to give a reason for refusing to enroll a child, you do need to comply with the state and federal laws on discrimination (see page 75). You cannot deny care because the child is from Korea or the parents are Jewish. You can refuse a child based on age, since the age discrimination laws apply only to adults.

Family child care providers are also required to abide by the ADA, which requires you to make "reasonable accommodation" to serve a child who has special needs (see below). You must make any accommodations necessary to provide care for the child unless doing so would create a significant difficulty or expense for you.

As long as you don't violate the antidiscrimination laws, you may choose to deny care for any reason. (For more information on discrimination, contact your child care resource and referral agency or consult the *Legal and Insurance Guide*.)

• •

Children with Special Needs

The ADA prohibits you from discriminating against children who have special needs. This means that you must make a reasonable effort to allow those children to participate in your program, unless doing so would create a "significant difficulty or expense." Because of this requirement, you cannot put a statement in your contract or policies that you won't care for children with disabilities, children on medical monitors, or children with AIDS, even if you qualify this by saying "children with disabilities for which I have no training," or other similar language. (You can describe any experience, skills, or training that you do have in caring for children with special needs.)

You cannot ask a prospective client if his child has a disability. After the child is enrolled you can ask whether the child has any special needs that you need to address. If the answer is yes, you can ask the client to provide you with written instructions for meeting those special needs. When a client tells you that his child has a disability, you cannot share this information with your other clients without his permission, preferably in writing. (For more information about ADA and caring for children with disabilities, see the *Legal and Insurance Guide*.)

Most family child care providers have probably cared for a child with special needs at one time or another. In most cases the key to successfully caring for a child with a disability is to maintain good communication with the child's parents and to ask for help from your licensor or local health care worker. Bear in mind that the experience that you gain caring for this child will help you promote your program to other clients who have children with disabilities and are willing to pay for high-quality care.

Complete a Trial Period

When you add a new family to your program, I recommend that you always start with a one- or two-week trial period. During this trial period either party can end the child care agreement at any time without giving any notice. This allows either you or the client to back out gracefully if the arrangement doesn't seem to be working out.

When you set up a trial period, you should describe it either in your contract or in a separate written, signed agreement; in either case, be sure to clearly state when the trial period will end (for more information, see page 28).

Sign the Contract

At this point both you and the client should be ready to make a commitment by signing the contract. You might want to include the trial period in your contract and sign the contract before the trial begins, but you should complete all the other steps described in this chapter before you sit down to sign the contract. (For more information about the issues involved in signing the contract, see the section that begins on page 39.)

CHAPTER TEN

Making Changes and Exceptions to Your Rules

Chapter Summary
This chapter explains when and how to make changes and exceptions to your agreements, to adapt to new circumstances. It also explains when you shouldn't negotiate with a client who wants you to change a term of your contract or policies.

You and your clients will be living with your contract and policies long after you select your rules, write them down, and have your clients sign them. For this reason, they need to be living documents that you can adapt to meet new circumstances and needs. At the same time, there still will be situations in which you will need to put your foot down and insist that your rules are followed to the letter. This chapter will discuss when and how to make changes and negotiate exceptions to your contract and policies, and the next chapter will discuss how to enforce your rules.

Changing Your Contract and Policies

When you make a change to your contract, you must put it in writing and have it signed by the client in order to make it enforceable. If you don't do this, it can lead to problems. It's especially important to keep your contract up-to-date as you increase your rates and change your terms of payment during the year.

For example, let's say that you decide to change your contract to require your clients to pay you one week in advance. You tell them on December 1 that the change will be effective on January 1, but you don't draw up a new contract. When you ask for the extra payments on January 1, one of your clients says that she never received a new contract and won't make the advance payment until you produce one. To get her to pay you for the extra week, you'll have to sit down, write up a new contract, and have everyone sign it. To avoid this problem, give your clients written notification of any changes to your contract, and have them sign the new contract term when you announce it.

Here's another scenario: In March you tell your clients that you will be raising your rates effective April 1—but then you procrastinate and don't revise your contract. Your clients start paying the higher rate in April; in July one of them leaves without giving you the two-week notice that you require. Unfortunately, you never got around to asking her to pay for those two weeks in advance. If you try to enforce your contract now, you will only be able to sue her for payment at your lower March rate because you didn't put the contract change in writing.

If your policies are part of your contract, you'll need to follow this same procedure whenever you make changes to them. If your policies are separate from your contract, you'll be able to change them at will, unless you have agreed to give your clients notice before you make any changes. (If you use the worksheets on the CD to create your contract and policy handbook, it will be easy to type in your changes and print out a new agreement.)

You may also need to notify your licensor whenever you make changes to your contract or policies. Some states require licensors to keep a copy of these documents on file. Others only require you to update your licensor about certain changes, such as the list of people who are authorized to pick up the child. Ask your licensor whether or under what circumstance you will need to notify her about changes to your agreements.

• •

How to Make Changes to Your Contract

There are three ways that you can make changes to an existing contract; although there is no legal difference between the three methods, one of them is less prone to error and misunderstanding than the others:

- You can just strike through the old terms in the client's current contract and write in the new terms by hand. To make the contract change legally binding, have your client initial and date it.

- You can write a separate addendum or amendment to the contract. This is a short note that refers to the original contract and describes an addition or revision to it, such as: "This addendum amends the contract between Paul Parent and Sue Provider signed on January 3, 20xx. On page 1 the weekly rate is changed from $125 a week to $135 a week." Have the client sign and date the addendum, give him a copy for his records, and attach the original to his contract in your files.

- You can rewrite the contract and have your clients sign an entirely new document. When you use the worksheets on the CD to create your contract, it's easy to revise your terms, print out a new version, and have your clients sign it.

My recommendation is that you completely redo your contract whenever possible. An addendum may be lost or separated from the original contract, and there's more chance for error on it (such as forgetting to date the signatures). Handwritten contract changes are the most prone to confusion and misunderstanding.

• •

Review Your Agreements Regularly

The best way to make sure that changes to your contract and policies go smoothly is to sit down with each client on a regular basis to review their terms and any changes to them. This will promote communication and remind both parties of their responsibilities. If possible, do this every six months, and be sure to do it at least once a year. You can review a contract at any time; the most common times are on the client's anniversary date, at the end of the calendar year, or at the start of the school year.

Prepare for the meeting by reviewing the client's current contract and policies to make sure those documents are up-to-date. As you review them, check that you're following your own rules—if you have a written policy, you need to follow it; it's better to have no written policy than to have a written policy that you aren't following.

For example, if one of your policies states that you will take the children on a field trip every week and you aren't doing that, you should remove that statement or it may lead to problems later. A client may argue that since you aren't following your policies, she doesn't have to, either. You can avoid this kind of attempt to shift blame by regularly checking and updating your policies.

During the review meeting, explain any revisions that you are making to the contract. Before you ask a client sign the new version, you should also check to see if she wants to make any changes to the information for her child, such as adding a new name to the list of people who are authorized to pick up her child.

• •

You Can Change Your Policies at Any Time

You don't need to wait for a formal meeting to revise your policies. Let's say that you want to start allowing the children to bring a special toy from home on Mondays. You can give your clients advance notice of the change, or you can simply announce that the next Monday, children will be allowed to bring one toy from home, and give each client a copy of the new policy. If you originally asked your clients to sign your policy handbook (see page 68), you can print out a revised version and ask them to sign it. However, you don't need their signature to make the change.

• •

Raising Your Rates

If you've been in business for a while, you may have been surprised to hear at some point that another provider who has just started her business is charging higher rates than you are. This is especially likely to occur if you haven't been regularly raising your rates over the years. Many providers are hesitant to raise their rates and are uncomfortable with even discussing this topic with their clients. Some even feel intimidated when prospective clients simply ask them for information about their rates.

One way to handle any awkwardness about raising your rates is to put a clause in your contract that says you will raise your rates annually, even if the raise is very small (see page 45). You don't need to give your clients any reason for this annual rate increase. However, if you do feel the need to explain it, here are some points that you could make:

- *My expenses, such as food, toys, utilities, and insurance, have gone up this year.*

- *I have one more year of experience as a provider, and that enables me to offer higher-quality care for your child.*

- *I had some special business expenses this year (a swing set, a computer, and so on).*

Not surprisingly, your clients won't always be happy when your rates go up—but don't let that deter you. Bear in mind that most of your clients receive regular raises from their own employers, and over time they should also expect to pay you more for child care. If a client refuses to pay the higher rate as scheduled, you should tell him that you are ending his contract according to the termination clause.

Here are two more suggestions for increasing your income from clients:

- Instead of raising your rates, you might increase your fees or add new fees. As discussed in chapter 5, you might consider charging extra for registration, liability insurance, field trips, activity supplies, sick days, vacations, or holidays.
- You could also raise your rates for infant care only. Since the demand for infant care is greater, clients will pay more for it, and it will probably be easier to raise your rates for infants than for any other age group.

• •

What Are the Rates in Your Area?
Since it is illegal to discuss rates with your competitors, you aren't allowed to ask other family child care providers or child care centers what they are charging. Your best approach is to ask your child care resource and referral agency for information about the child care rates and fees in your community—the agency isn't a competitor, and its information is available to the public. You may also want to review the chapter on setting rates in the *Marketing Guide* and the chapter on price fixing in the *Legal and Insurance Guide* (which explains how to legally collect rate information).

• •

How often should you raise your rates? Most providers raise their rates no more than once a year (and some raise them rarely, if ever). I don't recommend that you put in your contract any limit on how often you can raise your rates. If an emergency arises, you want to allow yourself as much flexibility as possible. This means that in theory you could raise your rates as often as you like—however, in reality it usually isn't a good business practice to raise your rates more than once a year.

Compare Your Income to the Minimum Wage

One way to determine what your rates should be is to compare your hourly net income to the federal minimum wage, which was $5.15 per hour as of December 1, 2005. Most family child care providers earn less than this. Although you may not be able to immediately raise your rates to reach the minimum wage, you could make this a goal, and gradually raise your rates up to the minimum wage over the next few years.

Here's an example of how to compare your income to the federal minimum wage:

Income

Child	Income/week		Weeks/year		Annual income
1. Toddler	$125	x	50	=	$6,250
2. Preschooler	$115	x	50	=	$5,750
3. Preschooler	$115	x	30	=	$3,450
4. Preschooler	$115	x	40	=	$4,600
5. School-ager	$70	x	30	=	$2,100
6. School-ager	$70	x	20	=	$1,400
7. School-ager	$70	x	25	=	$1,750
Food Program Income					$3,000
Total Income					**$28,300**

Expenses

Food	$3,500
House expenses	$3,450
Business liability insurance	$700
Car expenses	$800
Supplies/toys	$3,000
Household items	$1,300
Depreciation	$1,000
Taxes	$2,800
Total Expenses	**$16,550**
Net Income (profit)	**$11,750**

Your hours worked (including business activities when the children weren't present):
    55 hours per week x 50 weeks = 2,750 hours
Your hourly wage: $11,750 ÷ 2,750 hours = $4.27 per hour
Minimum wage: 2,750 hours x $5.15 per hour = $14,163

In this example the provider is earning $4.27 per hour (based on a profit of $11,750 and 2,750 hours of work). However, to earn the minimum wage of $5.15 per hour, she would need to make a profit of $14,163—or $2,413 more than she is making now ($14,163 – $11,750 = $2,413).

If we add up the weeks that each child is enrolled in her care per year, we come up with 245 weeks. If we divide $2,413 by 245 weeks, we get $9.85 per week. So to earn the minimum wage this provider would need to charge an extra $9.85 per child each week. This would represent about a 12% increase in rates for a full-time child.

In setting your rates, I encourage you to figure out how much you are really making per hour by dividing your net income by the total number of hours that you are working at your business. Remember to include the hours that you spend on business activities when the children aren't present, such as record keeping, cleaning, and preparing meals and activities.

Negotiating Exceptions to Your Contract and Policies

As we have seen, the terms of your contract and policies can be just about anything that you want; however, they also need to work for your clients. To meet their needs, your agreements can't be written in stone. You need to be flexible enough to respond to changing circumstances and be willing to negotiate a compromise when appropriate.

It's okay to negotiate a compromise when you and the client can talk openly and both sides are willing to give up something to make an agreement work. However, don't compromise your rules if you feel that the client doesn't respect your position or won't listen to you. Other than that, you should feel free to adjust the terms of your contract and policies as needed to satisfy a client, as long as the change won't create problems for your other clients.

If you have a problem and can't come up with any ideas for a compromise solution, you can ask your licensor or local child care resource and referral agency for help. Here are three examples of how you might negotiate your terms to keep a client happy without giving up what is most important to you.

Example 1: Jolie Likes Her Vegetables Raw

In this example, you enroll a new child, Jolie, and within a few days you discover that she is used to having three snacks a day, she likes her vegetables raw, and she has been bringing special treats from home every day. However, you serve two snacks a day, you cook all your vegetables because the other children prefer them that way, and you have a policy that children aren't allowed to bring treats from home. What should you do?

Your first impulse might be to just ask Jolie's mother to follow the rules of your program; but if you do that, she's likely to exercise her rights during the trial period and simply leave your care. You decide to try to avoid that outcome by seeing if you can negotiate a compromise that will work for both of you. You review the three issues and come up with the following ideas for a compromise:

- Three snacks: You explain to Jolie's mother that if you serve three snacks a day you will have to serve them to all the children, and you don't have the time (or the budget) to do that. Instead, you suggest that she serve Jolie a snack when they get home after your program. Or you offer to set aside some raw vegetables when you're making lunch and later serve all the children an extra "vegetable snack."

- Raw vegetables: You offer to set aside some raw vegetables for Jolie when you cook the vegetables for the other children. Or you suggest that her mother prepare some raw vegetables for you to serve Jolie and bring them each morning.

- Treats from home: You explain that you won't be able to compromise on this point because any flexibility in your rules about treats from home would create havoc with your other clients.

By breaking down the issues and providing suggestions for solving them, you have a better chance of keeping this client happy than you would by just telling her to follow your rules. This approach is also likely to impress her by showing that you can be both flexible and firm in implementing your policies.

• •

When a Client Asks "Why?"

When a client argues with you and asks, "Why do you have this rule?" the best response is, "Because that's my policy, and I've found that it works well for me." Some providers feel the need to explain and justify their rules because they want every client to see things their way—but that just isn't possible. If a client pushes you for an explanation, all you have to say is, "These are my rules." (If a client argues about your contract terms in the initial interview, this could be a sign of things to come and might be a good reason not to enroll the child.)

• •

Example 2: Will You Negotiate Your Late Fee?

Now let's look at a conflict that involves money: One of your clients complains about your policy of charging a $3 late fee for every fifteen minutes that a child is left in your care after the agreed-upon pickup time. How can you resolve this conflict?

You always have the option of taking the position that your contract terms aren't negotiable. In this scenario, you might let the client have her say, and then respond,

I'm sorry that we don't agree on this, but I'm going to enforce my late fee because I believe it's the best way to run my business.

Don't apologize for the terms of your contract or policies. There will always be clients who have unreasonable expectations. However, what if a client just asks if you can be flexible about enforcing your late fee? In this case, she may be testing you to see if you are serious, or she may have a real problem and be trying to find a compromise. You might be willing to work with her to negotiate a compromise; for example, many providers will bend their rules when a family is having a financial or health crisis.

So you might respond by asking the client to explain her specific problem and any compromise solutions that she might suggest. (If the two of you can't come up with a solution right away, put off the decision for a while, and ask other providers and your licensor if they have any other ideas. Remember, you always have the option of insisting that the client follow your rules.) Here are some objections that a client might raise to a late fee and some compromise solutions that you could suggest in response:

I can't make the 6:00 PM pickup time on Wednesday because I always have a late staff meeting on that day.

- I'll change your pickup time to 6:30 on Wednesday, and I won't charge you a late fee unless you arrive after that time; but on other days your pickup time will still be 6:00.
- We could raise your weekly fee by $4 to cover the extra half hour of care on Wednesday. This will cost you less than paying a late fee of $6 every week.

I can't afford to pay such a high late fee.

- What fee do you think would be reasonable for my time? [If the client doesn't have much money, you might want to lower your fee for this family.]
- How often do you expect to be late? [If it's often, you may not want to compromise with this client. If it isn't, you could do a one-month trial period without a late fee and then reassess that rule.]
- You can ask someone else to pick up your child when you know that you'll be late.

I don't have any cash to pay the late fee when I pick up my child.

- Bring your checkbook.
- You can give me a deposit at the beginning of each month to cover the late fees.
- I'll let you pay me the late fee the next morning—but if you fail to pay it by then, I will charge an additional penalty of $10 in addition to the late fee.

When you agree to compromise one of your rules, it's a good idea to do a trial period at first to see if you are really comfortable with the change. Let the client know that you are only agreeing to try it out and will make a final decision at the end of the trial period.

Example 3: George Can't Pay His Bill
In this example, George (a single parent) is getting behind in paying you his weekly fee of $130 because he's having money troubles. How should you handle this?

Although many providers are willing to help clients who are having short-term financial problems, you shouldn't get into the habit of carrying a client's debt for longer than a few weeks at the most. In addition, it may be counterproductive to charge a late payment fee if the client doesn't have the money in the first place.

One solution would be to ask George to pay you a little extra each week until he catches up. It's important to require him to pay you something on a regular basis, even if it's a small amount, so that he won't forget about the debt. You should also write up a debt repayment agreement for him to sign. For example, if he is behind by $260 for two weeks of care, this agreement could read:

George Smith agrees to pay $20 a week over his usual weekly fee of $130 for 13 weeks to repay the two weeks of child care (March 1–15, 20xx) that he hasn't paid for. His new weekly fee of $150 will begin on May 1, 20xx, and it will be due on Monday morning each week. If he fails to pay the $150 on time, the provider may either charge an additional fee of $10 a day for every day that the payment is late, or she may cancel the contract immediately.

Once George signs this payment agreement, you will be able to enforce it in court if it turns out that he doesn't fulfill his obligations. For example, if George shows up a few weeks later and says that he won't be able pay the new $150 fee after all, you can immediately enforce your $10 a day late payment fee—and if he still can't make his payments, you can stop providing care for his child. If you decide to take him to court for the money he owes you, you will probably win.

On the other hand, if you can see that George is really struggling, you may want to forgive his debt entirely and continue to care for his child anyway. If you do this, you should tear up the repayment agreement, then tell him that you aren't going to enforce his past due debt and would like to start over with a clean slate.

You can negotiate this kind of special arrangement with one client, and not offer it to any of your other clients. However, don't assume that the other clients won't find out about it. If another client asks why you have made an exception to your policies, you can say that you consider exceptions to your policies on a case-by-case basis when a client or a child have unique circumstances, and that it is your policy to treat all your clients the same in similar circumstances. However, you can't explain what those circumstances are without violating the first client's confidentiality.

• •

Don't Negotiate over Unacceptable Behavior

Don't negotiate with a client who regularly violates your contract and refuses to change his behavior. For example, let's say that your fees are due on Friday and you have a $10 per day late fee. One of your clients regularly waits until Saturday and then pays his regular amount plus the extra $10. However, you don't want to wait for your money, so you tell him that you're raising his late fee to $20 a day and you won't be waiting around on Saturday for him to pay you. He says that's unfair, since if you aren't around he might have to pay a $60 late fee on Monday.

Should you negotiate with this client? No; you are free to set your own rules. You can raise your late fee for one client if that's what it takes to get him to pay on time, and you aren't required to sit around over the weekend waiting for him to show up and pay you. You should tell this client to pay up on Friday or you will simply charge him a $60 late fee on Monday.

• •

When It Isn't Covered in Your Contract

No matter how carefully your write your contract and policies, unanticipated situations will arise that aren't covered in your agreement. For example, there is a death in your family and you close your business for two days to attend the funeral. Neither your contract nor your policies state whether your clients must pay if you close because of a funeral. Since your agreement doesn't address this situation, you can't require your clients to pay for the days you were closed. You could try to negotiate this with your clients by asking them to pay for one or both of the days. If they agree, then the problem is solved.

• •

Q & A: An Abusive or Disrespectful Client

Q: What should I do about a parent who uses abusive language and treats me with disrespect in front of the children? I provide wonderful care for his child, and I'd hate to see her leave.

A: Outside of the children's hearing, tell the client,

> *I won't allow you to use that kind of language around the children. If you do it again, I will ask you to leave the room immediately.*

Describe the specific behavior that is unacceptable ("I don't appreciate it when you say . . .") and the change that you are requesting ("I want you to stop saying . . ."). No matter how much you care about the client's child, it isn't healthy to accept discourteous treatment from a client. Insist on being treated with respect. If you don't get it, end the relationship.

• •

Whenever a new situation comes up, you will want to change your contract to explain how you will handle it. But what if a client raises an issue that isn't covered in your contract, and you aren't sure how to respond? For example, a client asks if you will care for her child who is suffering from a minor illness. You have a policy that you don't care for sick children, but when you wrote that policy you weren't thinking of a minor noncontagious illness. If you aren't comfortable giving an answer right away, you can ask the client to put her request in writing so you can consider it after business hours. You could also say,

> *I'll need to give it some thought; I'll get back to you later.*

Don't let a client pressure you into feeling that you need to rush into a decision that may have unforeseen consequences.

If a client wants you to make a change to your contract and you don't want to make that change, the client's only option is to give you notice and terminate the contract. Although you may want to avoid this, sometimes it won't be possible. For example, if a client says,

"I don't want to have to pay you when my child is sick, because then I have to pay double when I hire another person to care for her." If your contract says that clients must pay when a child is ill, and you don't want to change that for this child, you can tell the client,

> *I'm sorry, but our contract is clear on this point. If I let you do this, all the other clients will want the same thing, and I won't be able to afford to stay in business.*

If you aren't willing to negotiate this point, then enforce your rule and let the client decide whether to stay or not.

CHAPTER ELEVEN

Enforcing Your Contract and Policies

Chapter Summary
This chapter explains how to effectively enforce the terms of your contract and policies, including how to set consequences for unacceptable behavior. It also explains why the fear of losing clients shouldn't stop you from enforcing your agreements.

M any family child care providers feel that enforcing their contract and policies is one of the most difficult aspects of their job. When they start to feel anger and frustration with a client, many providers prefer not to deal with the conflict at all and simply hope that it will go away. Some don't speak up to a client because they are afraid that they might be wrong or that the client will get angry and terminate their agreement.

However, your contract and policies won't mean much unless both parties take them seriously and expect that the terms of the agreement will be met. This is true even if the client is a relative or close friend. You have made a contract that the client can enforce against you, and you should be prepared to enforce it against a client as well. If either party is allowed to ignore any of the terms of the agreement, it undermines the trust in the business relationship.

Take Your Agreements Seriously

A contract can't protect you unless you consistently follow its terms and insist that your clients do the same. For example, let's say that your contract requires your clients to pay you for ten holidays, but you don't actually enforce this rule for Christmas and New Year's. If you end up having to take a client to court for not paying you for the Fourth of July, you may lose. The client can argue that by not following your own holiday terms, you have led your clients to believe that it would not be enforced.

It is easier to enforce a written contract or policy than a verbal one. You can pull out a written agreement, point out a term to the client, and say, "This is what you agreed to do." However, many providers can't get up the nerve to do this. If you don't feel confident enough to take the initiative and directly confront a client, try these suggestions:

- Set up regular client meetings on a weekly or monthly basis (see page 14). You may find that it's easier to bring up a problem if you are communicating regularly.

- Write a note to the client pointing out the problem. "Yesterday, January 12, your child arrived without a hat or mittens, and she couldn't play outside. Please remember to bring them tomorrow." Give the note to the client directly; don't slip it in her diaper bag or hand it to the child.

- Discuss the problem with another provider, your licensor, or a friend (you can do so without violating your clients' privacy if you don't share their names). Ask for ideas about how to deal with the situation.

- Ask your local resource and referral service or another provider to sit down and mediate between you and the client.

Point Out All Violations

Use your contract and policies as a guide to acceptable behavior, and don't hesitate to point out all violations to their terms. In fact, it's a good idea to get into the habit of bringing up all violations of your contract or policies to show your clients that your rules are being consistently enforced.

For minor deviations, you can use the written agreement as a communication tool—when a rule is broken, take out a copy of your contract or policies and show the client the written rule that has been broken. If you are the one who is breaking a rule, tell the clients involved what you are doing to correct the situation. A simple apology may be all that is needed to keep things running smoothly.

When a problem arises, try to talk it out. Schedule a meeting at a time and a place where you won't be disturbed. Before the meeting, think through what you want to say, and write out the main points to help you remember them.

To keep the discussion from becoming personal, stick to the primary issue and relate it to a specific term in your written agreement. When talking to the client, control your emotions and keep the children out of the dispute. Also, focus on the client's behavior, not her attitude. You may feel that she has a bad attitude toward life, but what you really want is for her to pay you on time instead of two days late. Listen to her problems, but be clear about what you want her to do.

That approach may be all you need to resolve minor problems. However, if the client's violations are serious or repeated, it's time to lay down the law:

> *Ellery, this is the second time you've picked up your child late this month. Our contract calls for you to pay a late fee when this happens. I haven't asked for payment until now, because I've tried to be flexible about your schedule. However, as of next Wednesday, I will start enforcing our contract. Do you understand?*

If you find yourself in a situation where you haven't been consistently enforcing your rules, it's never too late to start doing so, as shown in this example.

• •

Dad's New Girlfriend

Sometimes you will have to make up a rule before you can enforce it. Here's an example: The parents of a child in your care are divorced. The mother has custody Monday through Thursday and the father has custody on Friday. One week the father tells you that his new girlfriend will be picking up the child starting next week. The mother hears about this, and tells you that she doesn't want you to let the girlfriend pick up the child. What should you do?

Although there may be no solution that will make both parents happy, you're in the middle of their dispute and you'll need to respond somehow. Basically, you have three options:

- You tell the parents that your contract allows parents to list the names of the people who are authorized to pick up their children. Therefore, the father has the right to give you the pickup list for his day and the mother has the same right for her days.

- You tell the parents that you don't want to be in the middle of this conflict and they must agree on the pickup list for each day of the week. Tell them that if they can't agree, you will choose option one or three.

- You make your own decision about whether to allow the girlfriend to pick up the child on Friday.

• •

What Are the Consequences?

In order to enforce the rules of your contract and policies, there must be consequences for not following the rules. When a client violates your contract, the most common consequence is to charge the client more money, and the ultimate consequence is to terminate the client's contract. It's as simple as that. I'll use an example to illustrate this.

Josh brings his child to your program only on Fridays and pays your hourly drop-in rate. However, there are some weeks when he doesn't show up or give you any notice that he won't be coming. When you ask him about this, he says that he took the child to her grandmother's house that week. You tell Josh that he needs to give you notice when he won't be bring the child to your program, but his behavior doesn't change. If your words don't have any effect, your only recourse will be to tell him that you will establish one of the following consequences:

- You will charge him for a full day if he doesn't call you to cancel by 8 PM the night before.
- You will terminate the drop-in care arrangement for his child the next time he doesn't bring her to your program as scheduled.

Here's another example: Providers often complain that clients leave owing them money—but let's say that your contract simply states,

Clients must give a two-week notice before removing their child from care.

This language won't prevent a client from leaving without notice, since it provides no consequences for failing to give notice. What will happen if a client does leave without giving notice? Since this contract doesn't say that the client is required to pay for those two weeks, it will be difficult to enforce that rule in court. Your contract should specify that the client is required to pay for the notice period:

Clients must give a two-week notice before removing their child from care. Payment is due for the two-week notice period, whether the child is brought to the provider for care or not.

Most family child care clients aren't bad people who are looking for ways to violate your contract or give you a hard time. However, your clients aren't responsible for enforcing your agreements—you are.

Providers who set clear rules and establish specific consequences for failing to follow those rules generally have very few problems with their clients. In fact, many clients prefer their provider to set clear boundaries, because it lets the client know what to expect. The providers who have the most trouble with their clients are those who either don't set clear rules or who are inconsistent about enforcing the rules that they have set.

• •

Who Is Responsible for the Consequences?

Sometimes a client may argue that she isn't responsible for the actions of another person. For example, the parents of a child in your care are divorced; the mother has legal and physical custody, and the father is reimbursing her for part of the child care expenses. The mother allows him to pick up the child on Mondays, but he regularly shows up late.

When you ask him to pay your late fee, he says that he doesn't have to pay anything because he never signed your contract. So you ask the mother to pay, and she refuses to pay any fees that he has incurred. What should you do?

Since the mother signed the contract, she is responsible for paying the late fees. If she wants the father to be obligated to pay these fees himself, she needs to convince him to sign your contract. If he is unwilling to sign it, she must pay your fees herself and try to get him to reimburse her.

The answer would be the same if the parents were happily married and a friend picked up the child on their behalf and showed up late. The person who signs the contract is the one who is responsible for its consequences.

• •

● ●

You Can Still Choose Not to Enforce Your Contract

Despite everything I'm saying about respecting your own rules, there still may be times when you deliberately choose not to enforce your contract. For example, let's say that after a month in your program a client comes to you and says,

> *I think I made a mistake by putting Jana in child care so soon. I miss not being with her all the time, and I've decided to quit my job and stay at home with her for a while. I know that our contract requires that I give you a two-week notice, but I wonder if you'll waive this rule for me?*

Although you're free to require this mother to pay you for the two weeks, you may decide not to enforce your contract if you can see that it would be better for the baby to stay at home with her mother. One of the benefits of being your own boss is the freedom to make decisions that are in the best interests of the children as well as yourself. Don't feel guilty about making an exception when it's truly warranted.

● ●

What If Clients Leave Your Program?

Some providers are afraid that if they enforce their rules, their clients will leave. This fear can paralyze you and make it difficult to run a successful business. Ultimately, if you don't feel that you can enforce one of the rules in your contract or policies, then you should take it out. Otherwise you don't have rules, you just have guidelines—and by not enforcing them you run the risk of undermining the effectiveness of the rest of your rules.

When I do family child care contract workshops across the country I ask the participants, "What's the worst thing that could happen if you enforce your rules?" They tell me that their worst fear is that a client will leave their program. Then I ask, "How many of you have actually lost clients because you enforced your rules or raised your rates?" Usually there will be some hands in the air. Then I ask, "How many of you feel that you made a mistake and wish those clients had stayed with you?" In over twenty years of asking that question, I have seen only one provider keep her hand up and say that she regretted her choice.

This is telling. Although many providers are afraid of enforcing their rules, almost all of those who do enforce their rules come to believe they have made the right decision. Most clients will expect you to enforce the rules of your contract and policies and will be more comfortable with you if you do. Also, most of them aren't looking for reasons to leave your program (if they are, it may be best to let them go).

If you're doing a good job of communicating with your clients and are offering a high-quality program for their children, you don't need to worry about what will happen if you enforce your rules or raise your rates, even if your clients complain about it. And if a client does decide to leave for that reason, the cumulative experience of your fellow providers across the country shows that you won't regret it in the long run.

The Three Choices

When you're having a conflict with a client, there is a simple but effective technique that I have developed to help you decide how to handle it—I call it "the three choices of life." The three choices are:

- I am happy—I can agree with what the client wants to do.
- I am unhappy—I will tell the client what she needs to do differently, and if she doesn't change her behavior, I will terminate her from my care.
- I will shut down my business.

To use this tool, you will need a coach; this person can be anyone—your spouse, another provider, or a friend. The coach's job is to keep you focused on choosing one of the three choices to resolve your problem. Here's an example of how to use this tool:

Ella calls your home five times a day to talk to her child. You feel that this is disruptive, and you want to limit her to one call a day. You have discussed this with her, but can't come to an agreement. So you call your friend Linda, who has agreed to be your coach, and ask for her help. The two of you have the following dialogue:

Coach: "You need to make a choice. First, you can decide to let Ella call your home five times a day and not worry about it. Can you tell yourself that it's not that important to argue about this? Would that be acceptable to you? Could you be happy about this?"

You: "No. That's not an acceptable solution."

Coach: "Okay. If you aren't happy with this situation, then you need to decide what is acceptable to you. If you are only willing to have Ella call once a day, then you need to tell her that she gets only one call. If she continues to call more often than this, you need to terminate your contract with her. Could you do this?"

You: "But I enjoy caring for Ella's child and I don't want to lose her. I don't want to terminate her over this issue."

Coach: "You have one more choice, and that is to shut down your business. Are you prepared to do that?"

You: "No, of course not."

Coach: "Then you must be happy, and you should let Ella call as often as she wants."

You: "No, I don't want that."

Coach: "Then you must enforce your rule and terminate Ella's contract if she won't follow it."

As your coach, Linda's job is to keep running through these three choices until you finally decide on a course of action, because there are no other options. In the end, it isn't worth it to remain unhappy about a conflict with a client. You must either let the issue go, enforce your rule, or go out of business.

It isn't acceptable to say, "I'm unhappy, and there's nothing I can do about it." No matter what you say, your coach should keep steering you toward one of the three basic choices (whichever one you prefer; the coach should let you do the choosing). If you're having a hard time deciding what to do, you can always choose the first choice and meet again in a week to reevaluate the situation.

Most providers get stuck on the second choice. They admit that they are unhappy, but they don't know how to resolve the situation. To move forward, think carefully about what you would need to be happy. Focus on the specific action that the client would need to take—call only once a day, bring a change of clothes on Monday, pay on time, and so on.

If you decide to ask a client to change her behavior, be specific; don't make a vague request, such as, "Treat me with respect" or "Be more reliable." Also, be sure explain the consequences if the client's behavior doesn't change.

Usually the consequence for not following your rules will be termination, but there will be times when money may make a difference. For example, you might be willing to put up with five phone calls a day from Ella if she paid you an extra $25 a week. If so, you could propose this to her as a solution.

I believe that it is acceptable to pick any of the three choices. The only option that isn't acceptable is to be unhappy and not do anything about it. You may have allowed your clients to occasionally bend your rules and not let it bother you—life is too short to worry about everything. However, if the stress of dealing with your clients is so bad that you aren't happy and can't find a way to resolve your conflicts, then it's time to consider quitting child care and look for some other line of work.

CHAPTER TWELVE

Terminating a Contract

Chapter Summary
This chapter discusses how contracts are typically terminated and describes the steps that you can take to try to resolve disputes before terminating a client's contract. It also explains how to terminate the client if those attempts are unsuccessful.

This chapter discusses the issues related to terminating your contract. A contract may be terminated either by the client or by the provider. In some extreme cases it is even acceptable to terminate a contract immediately, without giving notice. Although you won't always be able to satisfy every client, if you follow the guidelines in this chapter I believe that you will be able to handle the termination process without unnecessary bad feelings.

When the Client Wants to End the Contract

You should anticipate that in most cases it is the client who will decide to end your relationship, even if you have been doing a good job. Although a client doesn't need to give you a reason for leaving, the most common reasons are that she is changing jobs or moving to another town or that the child is growing older. When a client leaves your program on good terms, ask her to fill out an evaluation form to give you feedback about your program and ask her if you can use her name as a reference for prospective clients.

If a client is leaving because she is unhappy, in most cases you won't be surprised when you receive her notice. Your regular meetings, discussions, and attempts to find a compromise should have revealed that there is a unresolved problem. When you receive the client's notice, you could offer to discuss the problem once more to see if a solution can be found. Otherwise, remind the client, if necessary, about the termination period specified in your contract. Since the client may not give you a written notice as required by your contract, you should give her a termination notice to sign, to make sure that there is no misunderstanding. (See below for more information about termination notices.)

If a client leaves without giving you notice, make a note of your last conversation with the client and file it with her contract. Record the date and time, what she said to you, and what you said to her. For example:

Oct. 12, 20xx, 4:30 PM
Shania Smith called and said that she wouldn't be bringing Jorge to my program anymore because she was taking him to her cousin who is starting a family child care business.

I reminded her that under the terms of our contract she was obligated to give me two weeks' paid notice. She said that she couldn't afford to pay double for child care. I replied that she had signed a legally binding contract with me, and she said that was just too bad. I replied that if I didn't receive the money from her by next Friday, I would take her to small-claims court. She then hung up on me.

I then called my licensor, Jeni Foster, and told her about this conversation to pro-tect myself in case Shania decides to make a complaint about me.

It's important to keep careful records of your conversations about termination, especially if there is a dispute over money. If you end up taking the client to court, these notes will play an essential role in making your case to the judge (see chapter 13).

• •

Sexual Play

A client tells you that according to her child one of the other children in your pro-gram is instigating sexual play. She threatens to remove her child from your care unless you immediately terminate care for the other child. What should you do?

First, you should report what you have heard to your licensor. You need to take any allegation of sexual play seriously, because it could be interpreted as child abuse by your licensor or child protection agency.

As to terminating care, that is a tougher decision, and you will have to use your own judgment about what to do. You have the right to terminate any client—and if you have reason to believe that a child has acted inappropriately, you may want to do so. On the other hand, this may be a situation that can be resolved with profes-sional help and patience.

• •

When You Want to End the Contract

There may also come a day when you decide that it would be best to terminate a contract with a client. When should you consider terminating your contract? Most providers don't terminate a contract without good reason, and there are all kinds of possible reasons that you might have for wanting to end an agreement:

- The client regularly breaks your rules.
- The client doesn't technically break your rules but is disruptive or difficult.
- The child is disruptive or difficult to manage.
- You would like to reduce your stress level by caring for fewer children.

In other words, you may just be too hassled to cope with the client or the child any longer. There is nothing wrong with terminating a contract to reduce your stress. You don't have to explain why you are terminating your contract, and you can do it for just about any reason, or for no reason, as long as you don't violate the laws against discrimination (see page 75). You can terminate a client because her payments have been late, she has bounced a check, she has made a complaint to your licensor, or simply because you don't feel like caring for her child anymore.

• •

When to Terminate Care Immediately

Regardless of the termination procedure outlined in your contract, there are some situations in which you should terminate a client immediately and not make any attempts at compromise or negotiation. You should do this if a client

- deliberately violates your contract or policies;
- falsely accuses you of child abuse or neglect;
- threatens you or your family;
- owes you money and refuses to follow a payment agreement.

Some providers are reluctant to terminate care because they feel an overwhelming responsibility for the child—but when a child's parents start behaving irresponsibly, at that point it is no longer about you or the child. When a relationship becomes unhealthy, you should end it right away.

Your clients also have the option of immediately terminating care if they have reason to believe that your program is unsafe or unhealthy for their child. A client once called me and asked, "My provider just informed me that she is going off the medications that she takes to control her violent emotions. Can I end our agreement without giving a two-week notice?" I told her to take her child home immediately. If your client has reason to believe that her child isn't safe in your care, a judge is unlikely to enforce the termination notice period in your contract.

• •

The decision to end an agreement with a client is never easy. Before you end your relationship with a client, you should try again to resolve the problem through discussion and negotiation (except in the extreme cases described above). Here are some suggestions for the steps you might take at this point:

Try to Resolve the Problem

As discussed in chapter 10, you will usually want to try to resolve the problem and negotiate a solution before you terminate a client's contract. It will be easier to resolve problems if you discuss each one with the client as it arises rather than letting problems accumulate until they reach a critical mass and tempers are strained.

When a problem or conflict arises, make it a habit to jot down some notes about what has happened (see page 18). You can use these notes to help you understand the problem and communicate more clearly with the client. Ask your licensor for suggestions about resolving the problem. If you can, also seek other outside help—a friend, nurse, or social worker might have some good suggestions. Don't assume that there is only one answer to the problem or that your solution is necessarily the best one. If you can be flexible about finding a solution, you will reduce your stress level and make it easier to solve the problem.

Try to Negotiate a Compromise

Don't be afraid to negotiate a win-win solution with the client—suggest ideas for a compromise that will allow both you and your client to get (at least part of) what you want: "What if we try your suggestion for saying good-bye to your child this week, and then my idea next week?" or "I won't charge you for your child's absence this week, if you're willing to pick him up a half hour early next Friday so I that can make a doctor's appointment." Remember, you can always set aside your rules and negotiate a unique solution for any client.

Give the Child a Time-out

Before you make the final decision to terminate a contract, you may want to ask the client to give the child a one-week "time-out" from your care. The idea is that a week away from your program may give the child a chance to relax and then get a fresh start. If you try this, don't charge the client for the time he is gone.

Steps for Terminating a Contract

Don't let it be a surprise to a client when you give him notice. If you are terminating care for your own reasons and the client hasn't done anything wrong, try to alert him to the possibility far in advance. For example, you might talk about reducing your program in your regular client meetings: "I've been struggling with whether or not I want to keep caring for this many kids." If the termination isn't the client's fault, you should always give notice—and make it as generous as you can—even if your contract allows you to terminate at will.

If you are terminating care because you are having a problem with the client, you should also make it clear ahead of time that you will be terminating care unless something changes. If you have failed to find a solution and the only remaining option seems to be to terminate the contract, I suggest that you follow these steps:

1. Clearly State the Problem and Its Consequences

Take the client aside and be very specific about what needs to change; state clearly that if the problem doesn't change, you will terminate your contract with him. Be very straightforward about the problem and its consequences:

> *Your checks continue to bounce, and although my contract doesn't include a bounced check fee and you do eventually pay me, I don't want to put up with this anymore. If this continues, it will be grounds for terminating our contract.*

If the client is violating one of the terms in your contract or policies, show him the specific language in your contract or policies when you have this discussion.

2. Give the Client a Written Warning

If the problem continues, give the client a written warning that his contract will be terminated if the problem occurs again. Give him a signed and dated note saying that this is his final warning and that you will terminate care if the problem occurs again:

> *We have discussed this, and your checks continue to bounce. This is a final warning to Francis Johnson that if his payment check bounces one more time I will immediately terminate our child care contract.*

3. Give the Client a Termination Notice

If the problem happens again, give the client a termination notice (see below). This notice should say that you are ending the child care contract. If your contract requires you to give a client notice when you terminate him, it should say that you are giving him notice according to the terms of your contract. If your contract allows you to terminate a client at will, you may want to take advantage of this option, especially if you feel that you have given the client plenty of warning and many chances to reform his behavior.

● ●

Watch What You Say

Be careful what you say in a dispute with a client. For example, what if you have a heated argument with a client, and your husband yells at him, "Leave our home!" Does this mean that you have terminated care? If the client doesn't return and you want him to pay you for failing to give you notice, it may be difficult to argue that you didn't give him notice. Although it may be difficult when you are angry, always tell the client that you are expecting him to bring his child to your program the next day, as usual.

● ●

Use a Termination Notice

When you decide to end a relationship with a client, it's important to carefully follow the termination procedure outlined in your contract (except in the extreme cases described in the box on page 127). You should give the client the notice period that is required by your contract, if any, and you should do so in writing, by giving him a termination notice. Here is a sample termination notice (also see the Forms section of the CD):

> *This note is to let you know that I will not continue to offer child care services to* _____ [child's name] *beginning on* _____ [date]. *I will continue to provide child care services until that date. According to our written contract, you are required to pay for my services until that date, whether your child attends my program or not.*

At the bottom of this notice, put lines for your signature and date and the client's signature and date. Sign two copies of the notice, and ask the client to sign one and return it to you for your records. If the client refuses to sign it, make a note on your copy of the notice that he refused to sign it.

If your contract says that you are allowed to terminate at will, you may terminate care immediately. If your contract doesn't say that you may terminate at will, you should follow the termination language in your contract. (For example, it may require you to give a two-week notice.) If your contract doesn't say anything about giving the client a termination notice, you may terminate immediately.

Keep your termination notice short and simple; don't include any explanation of why you are terminating the client. The client should already understand the problem and be aware that you are unhappy. Once you have reached the stage of sending a termination notice, restating the problem will only further aggravate the client. You just want to announce that you have terminated the client's contract and explain how the last days of child care will be handled.

Payment Issues during Termination

The termination process often leads to disputes about money. Here are some examples of the kinds of issues that can arise. Notice that most of these problems could have been avoided (or more easily resolved) if the provider had an advance deposit for the notice period (see page 47).

- A client gives you the two-week notice required by your contract and continues to bring her child to your program. Three days before the end of this period the two of you have an argument, and you tell her not to come back. If she has paid for the last three days, you should refund this money to her. If you are unwilling or unable to provide care throughout the notice period, the client shouldn't have to pay for those days.

- You give a client a two-week notice to end your contract. If the client finds child care after the first week, does she have to pay you for the last week? Yes. If she has paid in advance and voluntarily leaves before the end of the notice period, you aren't required to give her a refund, even if you have filled the space with a new child. (Although if you have filled the space, you could voluntarily give her a refund.)

- You and a client sign a three-week written notice, but you also verbally agree that she can leave earlier than this if she wants. After two days, she finds other care and leaves. You feel cheated, and want to change your mind. Legally you are still entitled to enforce the three-week notice, since your verbal agreement isn't enforceable—however, the client will be (justifiably) very angry if you do that, and may complain to your licensor. If you are feeling generous, consider the financial consequences carefully before you agree to make an exception for a client.

- A client has left owing you money; now she wants to come pick up her child's clothes and portacrib that she left at your house. Can you refuse to return her property until she pays what she owes you? Although you may wish to withhold her property to motivate her to pay you, there have been situations in which a client called the police and the provider was forced to return her property. If a client insists on getting her property back, I would give it to her to avoid the possibility of the police becoming involved or a complaint to your licensor about something more serious.

• •

The "Final Payment" Tactic

When an unhappy client leaves your program without a deposit to pay for the notice period, and you have a dispute about money, you may encounter the "final payment" tactic—the client may send you a check for some part of the disputed amount and write the words "final payment" on the memo line of the check.

If you cash his check as is, you are agreeing to accept that amount as the final settlement, and you won't be able to sue him later for the rest of what he owes you. If the amount is small, you may want to go ahead and cash the check and be done with it. Even if you have a good case, it may not be worth your time to pursue the client into court.

However, if you aren't willing to accept that partial payment as a final settlement, simply cross out the words "final payment" on the memo line and then go ahead and cash the check. That will allow you to continue to try to collect the remaining amount from the client.

You can use this tactic yourself to settle a financial dispute when a client has paid you a deposit and is arguing about her refund. Simply write "final payment" on your check to the client; if she cashes the check without crossing out your note, she has agreed to accept that check as your final payment.

• •

Handle the Notice Period Professionally

You should strive to maintain a professional attitude toward both the client and the child throughout the notice period, regardless of who ended the relationship. You might offer to give the client the number of the local child care resource and referral agency, so that she can look for another provider. Some providers give clients an album of photos of the child and the other children in the program to help ease the child's transition.

However, if you were the one who ended the relationship, the client may assume that you won't be able to treat her child with respect during the notice period, regardless of how professionally you handle yourself. Although this is unfortunate, it may be unavoidable. The best way to protect yourself is to make sure that the client has paid you for the last two weeks of care in advance (see page 47).

CHAPTER THIRTEEN

Taking a Client to Court

Chapter Summary

This chapter discusses three strategies that you can use to try to resolve a serious conflict with a client without taking the matter to court. It also describes how to prepare and make your case if you do try to enforce your contract in court.

Throughout this book, I have emphasized that a contract is a legal document that can be enforced in a court of law. This chapter will explain both how to resolve problems without going to court and how to enforce your contract in court, if that becomes necessary.

The vast majority of contract disputes between family child care providers and their clients never end up in court. Most of these problems are misunderstandings caused by poor communication or by failing to follow the practices described in chapter 2, and most of them can be resolved by taking the time to talk with your clients about each problem as it arises.

If a conflict with a client does turn into a major problem, your options for enforcing it depend on the nature of the violation. If the client has violated one of your policies, your ultimate option is to terminate the contract; you have no legal recourse, since your policies aren't enforceable by a court. However, if the client has violated your contract and owes you money, you have the option of taking her to small-claims court to try to get the money. However, this should be your last resort—first try to find a compromise solution, as described in chapter 10.

• •

The Best Way to Stay Out of Court

There is a simple way to almost eliminate the possibility that you will ever have to take a client to court—require payment at least one week in advance and get a deposit for the last two weeks of care when clients sign your contract (see pages 46–49).

• •

Try to Resolve the Problem First

If you have been unable to solve a problem through discussion, negotiation, and compromise, there are two more approaches that you should consider before you take the client to court—working with a mediator and sending a demand letter.

Try Mediation

Mediation is a voluntary dispute-resolution process that can help you and your client reach your own solution. Some communities have mediation centers that can provide a neutral mediator to help resolve a problem; the cost of this service is usually very low.

To find out if there is a mediation center in your area, contact a local legal aid society, law school, or bar association. If there is no mediation center in your area, you could ask another professional who has experience resolving disputes—such as a pastor, rabbi, or counselor—to serve as a mediator between you and your client. There are a number of advantages to giving mediation a try:

- Mediation may allow you to solve the problem more quickly than going to court.
- Working with a mediator is less intimidating than going to court.
- Unlike a court hearing, mediation is confidential.
- Since mediation avoids the adversarial atmosphere of a legal case, it can make it easier to be flexible and achieve a win-win solution where both parties get what they need.
- When both parties contribute to the solution, they are more likely to abide by it. (If you win a case in small-claims court, you may still have trouble collecting your money.)
- If mediation fails, you still have the option of going to court.

Although mediation is voluntary and neither party is obligated to follow the mediator's recommendations, you and the client may agree in advance that you will follow the mediator's recommendations. However, be sure to discuss this with your mediator in advance—some mediators don't make recommendations, they just help you find your own solutions.

• •

Try Offering a Final Compromise

When a client owes you money, you might try offering a final compromise, such as "Instead of immediate payment in full, I'm willing to accept $20 a week for the next six weeks." If the client won't agree to a compromise—or if she agrees, but doesn't live up to the agreement—then go on to the next step, sending a demand letter.

• •

If the client is unwilling to use mediation to settle the dispute and you decide to take the matter to court, be sure to inform the judge of this fact. It will increase your credibility because it shows that you tried to settle the conflict in good faith, and the other party refused to cooperate.

Send a Demand Letter

If the attempt at mediation fails, before taking legal action you should make a final written request for payment by sending the client a "demand letter." This letter should contain the following elements:

- The dates you cared for the child
- The amount the client owes you, and why
- A demand for payment by a specific deadline
- A notice that you will take legal action if the client doesn't respond by the deadline
- Your signature and the date of your signature

Before you send the letter, make a copy of the signed letter and put it in your file for that client. Send the original letter by registered mail so that you'll have proof that she received it. Here's an example of a demand letter:

> August 1, 20xx
> Lucy Stone
> 1453 Collier Ave.
> Garden City, Kansas 12345
>
> Dear Lucy:
>
> I provided child care services for your daughter, Mary, from January 1, 20xx, to June 28, 20xx; in 20xx, my fee was $135 per week. On June 28, 20xx, you informed me that you were leaving my program. At that time you owed me $135 for the week of June 24–28, 20xx.
>
> You did not give me a two-week written notice as required by the contract that you signed with me on January 3, 20xx. Therefore you also owe me $270 for the two-week notice period of July 1–12, 20xx, plus late charges, which are accumulating at the rate of $10 per day.
>
> I am requesting that you pay me the total that you owe me, $405, by August 15, 20xx. If I do not hear from you by then, I will have no choice but to take legal action against you. At that point I will file a claim in small-claims court for $405 plus late charges and court costs.
>
> (Your signature / date)

Sending a demand letter shows the other party that you are serious about collecting the money. The threat of a lawsuit may convince a delinquent client to pay, since most people don't want to be taken to court. Also, you can still decide not to take legal action, even after threatening to do so in the letter.

• •

Should You Use a Collection Agency?

Some family child care providers use a collection agency to try to recover the money that their clients owe them. However, this is expensive, since these agencies will either charge you a fee or take a large percentage of the money that they collect. Also, some of them won't take on a case unless you already have a legal judgment from a court. To find the collection agencies in your area, look under "Collection Agencies" in the Yellow Pages.

• •

Taking Your Case to Court

If the client doesn't pay you after receiving your demand letter, your only remaining option is to decide whether to pursue the matter in small-claims court. You may decide to drop the matter if the client doesn't have any money, the debt is small, or you don't want to take the time to appear in court.

If you do decide to sue the client, start by making the following preparations:

- Collect and make copies of all your records related to the case, such as your contract, your demand letter, and your notes about the situation.
- Write yourself a memo that describes the events leading to your decision to sue, so that you won't forget the details.
- Create a timeline of the dispute that shows all the relevant conversations, phone calls, letters, and other documents or events.

Filing a Lawsuit

Most states have a small-claims (or conciliation) court where people can bring lawsuits for small amounts, usually up to $10,000. This court is designed to be an informal and inexpensive way to settle disputes. In most states, the parties to the suit are encouraged not to bring lawyers. To find out how to file a suit in small-claims court, you can start by contacting your local county courthouse. However, you will probably need to file your lawsuit in person in the courthouse in the county in which the client lives, which may be difficult if the client has moved across the country. (In any case, you'll need to know the client's current address.)

The filing procedure usually follows this pattern:

- You complete a simple form in which you state that the client has violated your contract.
- You may have to pay a small filing fee. If you do, add it to the amount you are suing the client for.
- The court will usually notify you and the client by mail of the date and time of your court hearing. The time between the filing date and the hearing may be a few weeks or several months.

Be prepared for the possibility that when your client receives the notice of the court hearing, she may countersue you, claiming that it was you who violated the contract.

• •

Continue to Keep Your Licensor Informed

As when resolving disputes, continue to keep your licensor informed when you are taking a client to court. There is always a possibility that the client will make a complaint to your licensor at any time, and the best way to protect yourself is to stay in close touch with your licensor about any developments in the situation.

• •

Get to the Hearing Early

You should try to arrive at the courtroom at least twenty minutes before your hearing is scheduled to start. When you get there, look around the room and try to relax. If the client doesn't show up for the hearing, the judge (or referee) is likely to make a judgment in your favor.

If your client does show up, the judge may ask the two of you to try once again to reach a settlement before the case begins. If the client is willing, try to take advantage of this chance to work things out. If it doesn't work, you will be called before the judge, sworn in, and asked to tell your side of the story.

Make Your Best Case

The main thing to remember when planning your court appearance is that you will have a very short time in which to speak. This means that your testimony must stay clearly focused on the main point—the client has violated your contract.

Most providers are very nervous in this situation and don't do a good job of communicating clearly. To prepare for this possibility, it's a good idea to write out what you want to say in advance. Although it's best to explain your story to the judge in your own words, and only occasionally refer to your written statement, if you find that you are too nervous to do that, you can just read your statement.

Here's an example of the kind of statement you might prepare—it doesn't need to be any longer or more formal than this:

> *Your honor, I am Barbara Neilson. I provided child care for Mrs. Taylor for six months. Last November 1 she left my care without giving me the two-week notice required by our contract. Here is a copy of the contract she signed that requires her to give me a two-week notice when she leaves. I have asked her to pay for those two weeks. I wrote a letter asking her to pay. I asked her to go to mediation. She refused each time. I am asking the court to enforce our contract. Thank you.*

Here are some tips for making your best case in court:

Be Well Prepared
- Bring the timeline that you have prepared of all the conversations and events that are relevant to the dispute.
- Bring the originals and two copies of all the evidence you have collected—the timeline, the signed contract, any letters to and from the client (such as the demand letter), the notes of your conversations, the client's returned checks. (The first copy is for you, the second copy is for the client if she demands a copy, and the original is for the judge.)
- Offer the original documents to the judge. If she looks at them, she probably won't keep them. (But if she does, let her keep them; that's why you have a copy.) Bear in mind that a judge will never accept a copy of a document; you must produce the originals.

Stay Focused on the Facts
- Use notes to help you remember the most important points. You may only have one chance to tell your story.
- Stay focused and stick to the facts. Your case will be weakened if you ramble, forget, or are uncertain of the facts.
- If you would like a witness (such as another client) to testify for you, she must appear with you in court. Most small-claims courts won't accept a written affidavit.
- If the client has refused an offer of mediation, be sure to inform the judge.

What Your Client Might Say
When your client testifies, stay calm; engaging in a shouting match will weaken your credibility. If she makes statements to which you object, ask the judge if you may respond to those statements, and then do so as calmly as possible.

The client may bring up side issues to explain why she didn't follow your contract. For example, she might say,

> *I was unhappy with my provider because she wouldn't follow my instructions and make sure Joey didn't take a nap in the afternoon. This makes it very difficult for me to get him to bed at night.*

Don't argue about these stories, even if you know that they are false—her attempts to confuse the issue usually won't make any difference. Stick with the main point, that she has broken your contract. You might respond to her testimony by saying,

> *Your honor, I had discussions with my client about when her child should take naps. If she was unhappy with my policy, she had the right to remove him from my care, as long as she followed the terms of our agreement. She did not do so. A client shouldn't be able to get away with breaking a contract every time she's unhappy about something.*

If the client raises an issue that you've never heard before, be sure to point that out. You can say, "You never told me that before," or "You never complained to my licensor about that." If she accuses you of child abuse as an excuse for not paying you, quickly deny the allegations and tell the judge that your client's testimony is suspect since she never complained to you, to child protection, or to your licensor while the alleged abuse was going on. If she did complain, and your licensor determined that the complaint wasn't credible, be sure to point that out to the judge.

A client may be able to legitimately get away with breaking your contract if she can make a case that her child's health or safety was in immediate danger. For example, she might claim that you allowed the children to play in the street or that you were physically or emotionally abusing the children. However, these kinds of situations are very rare; usually when a client makes these kinds of allegations in court it's just an attempt to confuse the issue or get the provider in trouble.

How Will the Judge Decide?

Most small-claims courts will notify both parties of the judge's decision by mail within a few weeks after the court hearing. There is no guarantee that you will win your case, no matter what your contract says. If you are suing to get payment for days that you actually provided care to the child, you are likely to be awarded the money.

However, it is more difficult to get a judgment that a client must pay for the two-week notice period. You are more likely to win if your contract specifically says that your clients must pay for the two-week notice period, whether or not the child is in your care. If your contract simply states that "Clients must give a two-week notice," you are less likely to win, since the consequences aren't spelled out (see page 120).

Even though judges don't always enforce the two-week notice period, they should. Your contract should be binding unless there are unusual circumstances, such as the health or safety issues mentioned above. Unfortunately, some judges don't treat family child care with the same respect as any other business. Still, this shouldn't stop you from pursuing your case in court.

If You Win

If you win, the court will notify the client that she must pay you within a specific time period, usually no more than 30 days. If she doesn't pay you, it will be up to you to pursue her for payment. Ask the clerk at the small-claims court about collection procedures.

As a rule, that process will involve going to the sheriff's office in the county where the client lives and showing them your court judgment. In most cases they will charge you a small filing fee and you will need to provide the information necessary to collect the money, such as the client's bank account number or her place of employment. (This is why it's important to ask for a place of employment in the first section of your contract and to save copies of your clients' checks—see pages 34 and 45.)

The sheriff may be able to seize the money from the client's paycheck or bank account or place a lien on her house (so that she won't be able to sell the house until she pays you). In other cases, the sheriff may not be able to do anything to collect the money. However, once you file the paperwork, it's usually good for 10 years, and although it may take some time, you are likely to get the money eventually.

If You Lose

If you lose your case, try not to be too discouraged. Here are some coping strategies that may help:

- Try to accept the fact that the justice system isn't perfect and that some things happen that aren't fair.
- Think of this experience as an opportunity to learn how the legal system works so that you will be better prepared the next time.
- Rework your contract to avoid a recurrence of the same problem. Talk with your other clients to make sure that your agreements with them are clear.
- Write a letter to the client and describe everything you are angry about, as savagely as you want. Put the letter in a drawer and don't send it.
- Maintain your sense of humor and perspective. Life is too short to worry about a relatively small amount of money that won't enable you to retire any earlier.

Hiring a Lawyer

In most states you have the option of appealing the decision of a small-claims court within a short period after you receive the notice from the court. Ask the clerk at the small-claims court about the process for appealing the decision. These appeals are typically handled by an attorney and involve significantly higher filing fees than a case in small-claims court. (You might also need to hire a lawyer because of some other kind of contract dispute, or if you are sued over a personal injury or property damages.)

Like many people, most family child care providers have had little contact with lawyers, so finding one to represent you can be a challenge. If you are sued, first check your insurance policies to see if you are entitled to receive any legal assistance. Ask around for the names of attorneys who have handled cases similar to yours—for example, talk to your tax preparer, insurance agent, child care resource and referral agency, the local bar association, your friends, and other family child care providers.

Once you have the names of some attorneys, shop around as you would for any other service. Ask each attorney for fifteen minutes to discuss your problem. Many attorneys won't charge you for a first consultation. Meet with at least three of them, if you can. Ask them for references; call their references and ask how satisfied they were with the attorney's work. When deciding whether to hire an attorney, consider these criteria:

- Fees: Ask up front what the attorney would charge for a case like yours. Some attorneys charge by the hour; others work for a fixed fee.

- Compatibility: Pick someone you feel comfortable with and can easily talk to.
- Experience: Has the attorney handled other cases like yours?
- Location: Is the attorney's office convenient to your home?
- Size of firm: Smaller law firms sometimes charge less than large firms.

When you meet with an attorney, bring all the documents you have collected about your case, and try to be as clear as you can about your problem. Once you have chosen an attorney, put the agreement in writing and read it carefully—after all, you're signing another contract! (For more information about working with a lawyer, see the *Legal and Insurance Guide.*)

Final Words

In 1994 the Families and Work Institute published a report on children in child care. The researchers studied the quality of child care in three settings—regulated family child care, unregulated family child care, and relative care. Their test results showed that regulated family child care providers had the highest quality of care. Also, most of the clients interviewed in the study said that if their family child care provider asked them to pay more, they would do so rather than look for another provider.

According to this report, clients want their children to have high-quality care. They are looking for providers who are both sensitive and businesslike—and they see no contradiction between these two traits. Ultimately, if you set clear contracts and policies for your clients, communicate with them regularly, and consistently enforce your rules, you will attract and retain clients who will respect your business. The key to dealing with your clients is setting limits and sticking to your agreement. You are running a business, and must make the decisions that will enable you to provide high-quality care and support your family.

This book explains how you can use a written contract and policies to communicate more effectively with your clients so that you have more time to concentrate on your primary job of caring for children. However, it may not be easy to adopt all the recommendations in this book at once. You should move at the pace that feels comfortable to you. For example, you may want to start by asking your clients to sign a short written agreement. As you gain more experience and confidence, you can adopt a more detailed contract and policies.

It has been my intention in this book to empower you to more successfully manage your business and deal with your clients. I believe that by doing that you can improve the happiness of everyone involved—the children in your care, their parents, you, and your family.

If you have any questions about this book or any suggestions about how it could be improved, please contact me at tom@redleafinstitute.org or 651-641-6675.

APPENDIX A

Sample Contracts

Sample Contract 1: Basic Contract

Child Care Contract

1) This contract is made between Louise and Robert Brown (parents) and Jennifer Nelson (provider) for the care of Rebecca Brown (child), birthdate 2/12/04, at the home of the provider.

2) Child care will be provided from 7:00 AM to 5:30 PM.

3) The child care fee will be $135 per week, to be paid one week in advance. Payment will be due each Friday for the next week of care.

4) This contract may be terminated by the parents by giving a two-week written notice. The provider may terminate the contract at will. The parents will pay a $270 deposit that will cover the last two weeks of care, even if the child care rates are higher at that time.

5) The parents' signatures on this contract indicate that they agree to abide by the provider's written policies. The provider may change these written policies at any time.

Provider: Jennifer Nelson
　　Home address: 1567 Oden Court, Columbus, Ohio 44589
　　Phone: 675-895-3322
　　Cell phone: 675-188-9844
　　E-mail: littleducks@yahoo.com

Parent/guardian: Louise Brown
　　Home address: 45 N. Broadway Ave, Columbus, Ohio 44589
　　Business phone: 675-321-7664, ext. 44
　　Employer's name/address: Brown Electronics,
　　　56 W. 12th Ave., Columbus, Ohio 44609
　　E-mail: lbrown@comcast.net

Parent/guardian: Robert Brown
　　Home address: same as above
　　Business phone: 675-330-4988
　　Employer's name/address: Methodist Hospital,
　　　456 First Ave., Columbus, Ohio 44398
　　E-mail: lbrown@comcast.net

Parent/guardian signature　　　　　　　　　　　　Date

Parent/guardian signature　　　　　　　　　　　　Date

Provider signature　　　　　　　　　　　　　　　Date

Sample Contract 2: Child Care Agreement Form

Provider-Parent/Guardian Child Care Agreement

The following agreement is made between:

1. **Maria Hernandez-Mayer** — Home Phone: **555-1930** — Work Phone: **641-1241**
Mother/Legal Guardian
2654 Sherwood Ave., St. Paul, MN 55104 — E-mail Address: **mmayer@aol.com**
Home Address
Law Offices, Snelling Bldg. #65, St. Paul, MN — Cell Phone: **555-8643**
Employer's Name and Address

and

2. **Tom Mayer** — Home Phone: **555-1930** — Work Phone: **788-1452**
Father/Legal Guardian
same as above — E-mail Address: **Tmayer@aol.com**
Home Address
Northland Electric, 712 W. 7th, St. Paul — Cell Phone: **555-8657**
Employer's Name and Address

and

3. **Lynn Wyman** — Phone: **541-3252**
Child Care Provider
3624 Clearwood Ave., St. Paul — E-mail Address: **Lw102@hotmail.com**
Address / Cell Phone

for the care of:

4. **Danielle Mayer, 6/18/04** ; _____ ;
Child's Name/Date of Birth — Child's Name/Date of Birth
Joseph Mayer, 4/17/03 ; _____ .
Child's Name/Date of Birth — Child's Name/Date of Birth

Basic Rates and Payment Policies:

The payment fee shall be $_____ per month or $ **280** per week or $_____ per day or $_____ per hour.
Care shall be provided normally from **7** AM to **5** PM on these days: (Circle all that apply)

(Monday) (Tuesday) (Wednesday) (Thursday) (Friday) Saturday Sunday

Additional Fees (registration fees, bounced check fees, late payment fees, damage caused by children, etc.):

(fee is $140 a week for each child)

Payment shall be due on: **each Friday morning for the next week**

Overtime Rates:

1. For the purpose of this agreement, overtime will be considered as drop-off before **6:45** AM/____ PM and pickup after ____ AM/ **5:15** PM.
2. If the parent/legal guardian makes prior arrangements with the provider, the child may stay overtime at the following rate: $ **1** per **Minute** _____ or portion thereof.
3. If the parent/legal guardian has not informed the provider that he or she will be arriving earlier or later than the agreed upon times, the following rate will be charged: $ **1** per **minute** _____ or portion thereof.

Sample Contract 2: Child Care Agreement Form (continued)

Rates Regarding Holidays, Vacations, and Other Absences:

1. The following are paid holidays: *New Year's Day, Memorial Day, 4th of July, Thanksgiving, Christmas*

2. Charges for a child's absence will be: *each child will not be charged for 5 days a year for absences due to illness or family emergency*

3. Charges related to the provider's illness or other emergencies that prohibit care will be: *No charge*

4. Charges related to the provider's scheduled vacations are: *Parent will pay 1/2 of regular weekly rate for 2 weeks of provider vacation*

5. Charges related to the parent/legal guardian's scheduled vacations are: *Parent will pay regular weekly rate for any parent vacation*

The provider and the parent/legal guardian will each give _*4*_ weeks' advance notice of scheduled vacation or other leave.

6. Other: *Parent will pay regular fee when provider takes 2 professional training days a year.*

Other Charges:

1. There will be an extra charge for the following infant supplies when not provided by the parent/legal guardian: *disposable diapers*

   diapers, wipes, baby food, formula, etc.

   and for activity fees/expenses for: *swimming lessons*

   field trips, children's classes, materials for special projects, etc.

2. Care will begin on *1/4/07*. A holding fee/deposit of $ *250* is required to be paid on *10/1/06*, which will (will not) be applied to the first _____ weeks' payment. This is a nonrefundable fee.

3. The parent/legal guardian will pay in advance for the last two weeks of care by: *2/10/07*.

Termination Procedure:

This contract may be terminated by the parent/legal guardian by giving _*2*_ weeks' written notice in advance of the ending date. Payment by the parent/legal guardian is due for the notice period, whether or not the child is brought to the provider for care. The provider may terminate the contract (without giving any notice) or may give a _____ weeks' written notice. Failure by the provider to enforce one or more terms of the contract does not waive the right of the provider to enforce any other terms of the contract.

Signatures:

By signing this contract, the parent/legal guardian agrees to abide by the written policies of the provider. The provider may amend the policies by giving the parent/legal guardian a copy of the new or changed policies at least _____ days/weeks before they go into effect.

Provider's Signature _____ Date *10/1/06*

Mother/Legal Guardian's Signature _____ Date *10/1/06*

Father/Legal Guardian's Signature _____ Date *10/1/06*

Cosigner's Signature _____ Date _____

If the parent or legal guardian is under age 18, a cosigner must sign this agreement and act as a guarantor to the contract and agree to be bound by all financial terms.

Sample Contract 3: Fully Customized Contract

Child Care Contract

1. Names of the Parties to the Contract

Name of child care provider: Jennifer Nelson
Address: 1567 Oden Court, Columbus, Ohio 44589
Phone: 675-895-3322
Cell phone: 675-188-9844
E-mail: littleducks@yahoo.com

Name of parent/guardian: Louise Brown
Address: 45 N. Broadway Ave, Columbus, Ohio 44589
Home Phone: 675-479-3320
Work Phone: 675-321-7664, ex 44
E-mail: lbrown@comcast.net
Name/address of employer: Brown Electronics, 56 W. 12th Ave., Columbus, Ohio 44609

Name of parent/guardian: Robert Brown
Address: same as above
Home Phone: same as above
Work Phone: 675-330-4988
E-mail: same as above
Name/address of employer: Methodist Hospital, 456 First Ave., Columbus, Ohio 44398

Name of child: Rebecca
Date of birth: March 3, 2006

2. Hours of Operation
Hours of Care
The first day of care will be November 1, 2006. Rebecca's hours will be from 7:00 AM to 5:30 PM, Monday through Friday. (Late drop-offs do not allow for late pickups.) My program is open from 6:30 AM to 5:30 PM, Monday through Friday.

3. Terms of Payment
Rates
The child care fee will be $135.00 per week. You will pay this regular rate for summer vacation days, school vacation days, school snow days, school inclement weather days, and early school dismissal days.

Rate Increases
The child care fee will go up on November 1 each year.

Drop-in Rate
I do not provide drop-in care.

Payment Due Date
You will pay for child care one week in advance. Fees are due on Friday each week for the next week of care.

Late Payments and Insufficient Funds
You will pay a fee of $10 per day if you fail to make a payment on the scheduled day. The fee for an insufficient funds check is $10 plus any bank charges to my account.

Early Drop-off and Late Pickup
You will pay $1 per minute if you drop off Rebecca earlier than scheduled or pick her up later than scheduled. There will be no late fee for the first ten minutes after the scheduled pickup time. If you notify me of an early drop-off the night before, there will be no early drop-off fee. If you notify me of a late pickup at least one hour before the scheduled pickup time, there will be no late pickup fee. However, I may start charging for early drop-off and late pickup if you overuse these privileges.

Holidays
My child care program will be closed on the following holidays each year:

- New Year's Day
- Presidents' Day
- Martin Luther King Day
- Memorial Day
- Independence Day
- Labor Day
- Thanksgiving Day
- Christmas Day

You will pay the regular rate for these holidays. When a holiday falls on a Saturday, I will be closed on Friday. When a holiday falls on a Sunday, I will be closed on Monday.

Provider Absences
I will take 10 vacation days (two weeks) each calendar year. You will pay the normal rate for these vacation days. I will give you 14 days' written notice when I plan to take my vacation so that you can locate backup care. (You may also choose to pay 4% more than your regular rate [$140] for the other 50 weeks in the year and not be charged for my vacation days.)

I may take up to 10 personal days per calendar year. When I close my business to take a personal day, you will pay half the regular rate for that day. If I take more than 10 personal days in a calendar year, you won't have to pay any fee for the remaining days.

I may use my personal days for any personal or family needs, including (but not limited to) personal or family sick leave, funeral leave, or professional development.

Client Vacations

You may take up to five vacations days each calendar year and do not need to pay for child care on those days. You must give me four weeks' notice of the dates of your vacation.

Child Illnesses and Absences

You do not have to pay for five days per calendar year when Rebecca cannot come to care because of illness. However, you must notify me in advance (before the 7 AM starting time) whenever Rebecca won't be coming to care due to illness or any other reason. If you don't provide that advance notice, you will pay for the missed day(s) of care, regardless of any other terms in this contract.

Holding Fee

I agree to hold a space in my program until November 1, 2006, for Rebecca. In return, you agree to pay half my regular fee during the holding period. The fee to hold the space for four weeks will be $270, due upon signing this contract. This fee cannot be applied to the cost of care after Rebecca is enrolled. This fee is not refundable if you decide not to enroll Rebecca in my program before the end of the holding period. You must contact me two weeks before the end of the holding period to confirm that Rebecca will begin child care as scheduled.

Registration Fee

There is a registration fee of $25 for processing the paperwork required for enrollment and re-enrollment. You will pay this registration fee with the first scheduled payment after signing this contract.

Insurance Fee

I carry professional business liability insurance, and you will pay $25 twice a year toward the cost of this insurance. This fee will be due on the first regularly scheduled payment day after I receive the insurance invoice.

Field Trip Fees

There will be an extra fee for field trips. I will notify you of the fee for each trip at least one week in advance.

Fees for Extra Services

You will be responsible for bringing diapers, baby food, and formula to my program. If you do not bring these items, I will charge you for the cost of these items, and payment will be due at the next regular payment. If Rebecca breaks or damages my property, you will be responsible for paying to replace or repair the item.

4. Termination

Trial Period

The first two weeks in my program are an adjustment or trial period. During this time, either of us may terminate this contract immediately without written notice.

Termination after the Trial Period

After the two-week trial period has been completed, you must give me a two-week written notice if you wish to terminate this contract. I may terminate the contract at will without giving any notice.

Advance Payment for Last Two Weeks of Care

You will pay a $270 deposit that will cover your last two weeks of care, even if my rates are higher at that time. Since Rebecca will be starting care on November 1, 2006, you will pay this $270 on November 1, 2006.

5. Signatures of the Parties

By signing this contract, you acknowledge that you have read my policies and agree to follow them. I may amend my policies at any time by giving you a copy of the new policies at least two weeks before they go into effect.

If I fail to enforce one or more of the terms in this contract that does not waive my right to enforce any of the other terms of this contract.

_____
First parent's signature

_____
Date of signature

_____
Second parent's signature

_____
Date of signature

_____
Provider's signature

_____
Date of signature

APPENDIX B

Sample Policy Handbook

Child Care Policy Handbook

About Me and My Program

My Child Care Philosophy

I run a child-centered program that focuses on the individual needs of each child.

My Qualifications

I graduated from Oberlin College in 1985 with a degree in English. I have been a licensed family child care provider since 2000. I am currently working on becoming accredited by the National Association for Family Child Care and am a member of the local family child care association (Kerns County Family Child Care Association). I am certified in CPR and first aid.

My Licensing

I am licensed by the state of Ohio. A copy of my license is attached to these policies. My licensor's name is Phyllis Johnson, and you can reach her at 675-453-6000, extension 23.

I Am a Mandated Reporter

I am a state-mandated reporter of suspected physical or sexual abuse of children. This means that if I have reason to believe that any child in my care has been neglected or abused, I am required by state law to report this to my licensor or to the local child protection office. If you suspect that any child in my program is being physically or sexually abused, please talk to me immediately. If you wish to report suspected child abuse or neglect, you may contact my licensor or the local child protection office (675-456-8888).

Substitutes and Employees

I may hire a substitute caregiver in the event of an emergency or if I have an appointment that must be made during business hours. The substitute will meet all state child care regulations. If possible I will notify you at least a week in advance that I will be using a substitute caregiver.

My Privacy Policy

I will do all that I can to protect your family's privacy and will follow Ohio privacy law. I will keep all records and information about your child and your family private and confidential, unless I have your written permission to reveal specific information. I ask that you also respect the privacy of my family by not sharing any information you learn about my family without my written permission. I know that this can be difficult, so please talk with me if you have any questions about this.

Permission to Share Information

My first priority is to protect your child's health and safety. To ensure that I am operating with your full understanding and agreement, I ask that you grant me permission to conduct the following activities. Please initial each item for which you consent:

___ Placing photos of your child around my home.

___ Giving copies of photos of your child to other families in my care.

___ Placing photos of your child in photo albums that are viewed by prospective clients and other families in my care.

___ Using photos of your children in my marketing flyers.

___ Using photos of your children on my Web site.

___ Posting artwork and craft activities signed by your child around my home.

___ Occasionally involving the neighborhood children in indoor and outdoor activities with the children in my care.

___ Using an electronic monitor to listen to your child from another room.

___ Including the name of your child and the names of other members of your family in my client newsletter and posting this information on my bulletin board.

I Do Not Discriminate

I will not discriminate against any child, parent, or family for reasons of race, color, sex, age, disability, national origin, sexual orientation, or public assistance status.

The Rules of My Home

Please remove your shoes in my entryway before entering my home.

Your Responsibilities

Our Partnership

I expect that we will work together to ensure that your child has the opportunity to develop to his or her fullest potential. I expect that we will communicate often about your child's physical, emotional, social, and intellectual growth. Please inform me of any change in the child's schedule, routine, or home environment. I will do the same for changes in my business that affect your child.

You will provide any special instructions in writing for eating, sleeping or napping, allergies, health issues, toilet training, etc. You will also provide me with information such as an I.E.P. (Individual Educational Plan), guidance on your child's needs, and any other assessments needed for quality care.

You will also participate in a yearly evaluation of my child care program.

My Records for Your Child

I will keep the following records for each child:

* phone numbers for the child's parents, doctor, dentist, and emergency contacts
* a list of the persons authorized to drop off and pick up the child
* a signed and completed admission and arrangement form
* any special instructions from the child's parent/guardian
* immunization records that are updated:
  * every 6 months for infants.
  * every year for preschoolers.
  * every 3 years for school-aged children
* a signed consent form to obtain emergency medical care or emergency dental treatment
* written permission to transport the child

You must notify me as soon as possible if any of this information needs to be updated.

Backup Child Care Arrangements

You are responsible for finding backup care for your child when I go on vacation, become ill, or must close for any reason. You are also responsible for finding backup care if your child is ill. If you need the names of some caregivers who may be able to provide backup care, please talk to me.

Bad Weather Closings

You must notify me as soon as possible if your work closes early or is closed for the day. I will notify you as soon as possible if my program is closing or will be closed due to inclement weather.

Grievance Procedure

If you have any complaints about my program, please discuss them with me as soon as possible. If you have a serious complaint that you feel that I'm not addressing, you may wish to contact my licensor.

Child Care Program

Activities/Curriculum

I will conduct a wide variety of activities with your child, including: language development; sensory art activities; health, safety, and nutrition projects; puzzles; games; outdoor play; large muscle activities; free play; field trips; dramatic play; and more. All children's activities will be appropriate to the age of your child, which means they will be within the abilities of your child. I do not allow the children to watch television unless we are watching a specific children's educational program or viewing appropriate children's videos/DVDs.

Birthdays and Holiday Celebrations

I celebrate the birthdays of the children in my care on or near the date of their birthday. I ask that you not bring presents for these celebrations. We will also have a holiday party to celebrate Christmas, Hanukkah, and New Year's Day each year. You are asked to bring one small gift (less than $20 in value) to that party. The children will draw names out of a hat to determine which present they will receive. If you have any questions about what type of gift to bring, please talk to me.

Clothing

Please bring an extra set of clothing for your child, including shirt, pants, underwear, and socks. If your child is being toilet-trained, please bring two extra sets of clothing and a plastic sealable bag. All the clothing must be labeled with your child's name on it. During the winter, bring clothes for outdoor play, including a jacket, hat, scarf, mittens or gloves, a snowsuit or snowpants, and boots. During the summer, bring a swimsuit, towel, and sunscreen.

Food and Nutrition

I participate in a Child and Adult Care Food Program. You must sign a form to participate and must cooperate with requests for information from my Food Program sponsor. I serve the following meals:

- breakfast between 7:15 AM and 7:30 AM
- a morning snack between 10 AM and 10:30 AM
- a noon meal between noon and 1:00 PM
- an afternoon snack between 2:30 and 3:00 PM

You may not bring food from home into my program. I will offer the food to the children but won't make sure that they eat it. I will inform you if I notice any change in your child's eating habits. I will accommodate special dietary requests (vegetarian, nondairy, Kosher, food allergies, etc.). If your child has an allergy to food or drink, please notify me in writing. Copies of my menus are posted on my bulletin board.

Naps and Quiet Time

All the children will take a nap or observe a quiet time in the afternoon. All the children lie down during this time. Each child has his or her own clean and separate bedding, and you may bring a special blanket or other security item for your child. Children under the age of one year will sleep on their back to reduce the chance of Sudden Infant Death Syndrome (SIDS).

Toilet Training

I will use the following methods to help your child learn to use the toilet:

- giving the child incentives (stickers, etc.)
- bringing the child to the toilet instead of asking if she has to go
- using different methods to help the child get excited about using the toilet (dripping green food coloring into the water, sugar sprinkles, etc.)
- reading books and watching videos about learning to use the toilet
- creating a book for the child about their experiences

I will use the following terms while helping your child learn to use the toilet:

- Urine will be called "urine."
- Urinating will be called "urinating."
- A bowel movement will be called a "BM."

Toys

Toys may not be brought from home. I will not use toy weapons in my program (such as play guns). Your child will be taught to help pick up toys at the end of play time.

Children with Special Needs

Children with special needs are welcome in my program. I have experience and skills in caring for children with the following disabilities:

- ADD (Attention Deficit Disorder)
- physical challenges
- allergies
- asthma

If your child has a special need, please provide me with written instructions for providing special therapy, an individualized program of instruction, or behavior guidance. These instructions may come from you, a physician, a therapist, or another qualified person.

Behavior Guidance

I will not use any form of corporal punishment in my program. I will only use a "time-out" if it is age-appropriate for your child, and when I do, I will limit it to one minute per year of age. I will reinforce appropriate behavior by identifying the desired behavior rather than punishing negative behavior. I will use behavior guidance that is fair, reasonable, and suited to the age of your child. If your child exhibits a severe behavioral problem (such as regular biting, hitting, or breaking of toys), I will discuss this with you and ask for your cooperation in solving the problem.

Illness, Health, and Safety Policies

Sick Child Policy

I am not willing to provide care for your child if he or she is ill. I will not send a child home with a common cold unless it is accompanied by a fever or other symptoms. If your child becomes ill during the day, I will isolate your child from the other children and call you to pick up your child. I expect you to pick up your child within one hour of my call. I will notify you of any exposure to contagious illness, disease, or infection in my program within 24 hours of when I become aware of it. In the event of head lice, the child must be treated and nit-free before returning to care. If a case of head lice is found in my home, all parents will be notified and everyone in my home will be checked.

I expect you to notify me the evening before if your child will not come to care due to illness, contagious disease, or for any other reason. If a child has any of the symptoms listed below, he or she will not be permitted to attend care until 24 hours after the last bout of fever, vomiting, or severe diarrhea or until 24 hours after medical treatment has begun as prescribed by a physician:

- a fever of 100 degrees or higher
- a skin rash (other than diaper rash or prickly heat). The child will not be allowed to return to care without a written statement from a doctor that the rash is not a communicable condition.
- diarrhea (increased number and water content of stools that cannot be contained within the child's diaper)
- vomiting two or more times in a day
- any parasitic infestation (lice, scabies, etc.)
- pink eye
- discharge from the eyes or ears
- a runny nose with colored discharge
- chicken pox (The child may not return until all the blisters have dried and formed scabs, usually about 6 days after the onset of the rash.)
- any other communicable or contagious disease (such as tuberculosis)

Administering Medication

I will take children who are on prescribed medication when the doctor indicates that they are no longer contagious. Before I will dispense medication, I require a signed release from the doctor and a written request from you for each medical prescription. The medicine must be in its original container, labeled with the directions and the child's name. You should ask the pharmacist to divide the prescription into two containers, each with full labels, one for my home and one for your home.

Immunizations

You are required to keep your child's immunizations current and give me a copy of the immunization records for your child. I will notify you immediately if I learn that a child in my program does not have the proper immunizations. You must update my immunization records yearly.

Emergency Policy

I will call 911 for life-threatening emergencies. I will call you as soon as possible for all emergencies, whether life-threatening or not. If I can't reach you, I will call the other persons you have listed to call when you cannot be reached. I will post all emergency phone numbers near my telephone. I have smoke detectors and fire extinguishers that meet state law. I will report any accident requiring treatment by a physician to the proper agency.

You must keep me informed at all times of how I can reach you in the case of emergency (pager, voice mail, or cell phone), and check often for messages. If you will be leaving work early, be at another location for the day, or vary your normal routine, you must inform me.

Other Health and Safety Issues

- I do not have any pets.
- There is no swimming pool on my property, and my home is not near a lake, river, or body of water. I do let the children play in a wading pool in the summer.
- No one in my family smokes, and I do not drink during or before business hours.
- State law prohibits smoking in my home during child care hours, and my home is a smoke-free environment.

Policies for Transporting Children

Field Trips

I offer field trips as part of the educational program, and we may walk or drive on these trips. We may use my car, public transportation (bus), or other transportation. If I transport your child in a car, I will follow state law and properly secure your child. On each field trip I will carry a first aid kit and emergency contact numbers for all the children. I also have a field trip emergency plan.

During a typical year I will conduct field trips to the following locations: Stanley's Park, the playground at Mitchell Elementary School, the Lexington Library and Bookmobile, the local grocery store, and the playground at the First Baptist Church, as well as walks through the neighborhood. By signing my contract you are giving me permission to take your child to these destinations. If I take your child to any other destination by car, I will ask you to sign a written permission form.

Persons Authorized to Drop Off or Pick Up the Child

You must provide me with the name and a photo of each person who is authorized to pick up your child. You must notify me beforehand if an authorized person will be coming to drop off or pick up your child. Authorized persons who drop off or pick up your child must have identification available. I reserve the right to take anyone off the authorized pickup list for any reason. If a court order limits the rights of one of the parents, you must give me a copy of this court order.

Pickup and Drop-off Policy

In operating my child care business my first responsibility is to protect the health and safety of the children in my care. When you drop off and pick up your child, I want to make sure that the child is being transported safely. Transporting a child while under the influence of alcohol or drugs or without using an appropriate car seat creates an unsafe situation for the child.

If in my opinion a child cannot be safely transported to or from my home, I will ask you not to transport the child and will propose the alternatives listed below. If you refuse to agree to one of these alternatives and insist on transporting your child, I will immediately call the police and report the unsafe situation.

1. I will call someone to pick up your child from the list of people who are authorized to do so.
2. I will call a cab to pick up you and the child. You will pay the cab fare.
3. If you fail to bring an appropriate car seat for your child, I will ask you to drive home without the child and return with the appropriate car seat installed in the car. Under these circumstances I will charge a late pickup fee.

Transporting School-age Children

I will not pick up a school-age child from school due to illness. I cannot be listed as a contact in case of illness or injury during your child's school day.

Signatures

By signing this policy handbook, you indicate that you have read my policies and agree to follow them. When I make changes in my policies, I will give you a two-week written notice and ask you to sign the new policy handbook.

_____   _____
First parent/guardian signature   Date of signature

_____   _____
Second parent/guardian signature   Date of signature

_____   _____
Provider signature   Date of signature

About the Author

Tom Copeland is the director of Redleaf National Institute. He is a licensed attorney and has provided business assistance to family child care providers, tax preparers, and trainers since 1982. Tom is also the author of the *Family Child Care Record-Keeping Guide, Family Child Care Tax Workbook, Family Child Care Legal and Insurance Guide, Family Child Care Marketing Guide, Family Child Care Inventory-Keeper*, and the *Family Child Care Audit Manual*.

About Redleaf National Institute

Redleaf National Institute has been the leading educator of and advocate for the business interests of family child care providers since 1992. Our goal is to assist family child care providers in becoming successful in their businesses.

We Educate

Redleaf National Institute is the national expert on family child care business and tax issues. We help family child care providers and support organizations by keeping track of the latest tax changes, conducting research to find the answers to complex questions, and maintaining a database of resources. We share up-to-date information with the family child care field through training workshops, articles, and books, and provide individual business support via telephone and e-mail.

We Advocate

Redleaf National Institute works with individual family child care providers to help them resolve contract disputes with parents, protect themselves when investigated by regulators, defend themselves in IRS audits, find appropriate insurance, and much more. We also act as an advocate on behalf of the family child care field by lobbying the IRS and the U.S. Congress. For example, in 2003 our proposal to establish a standard meal allowance rate for family child care was accepted by the IRS in Revenue Procedure 2003-22, which greatly simplified the record-keeping and tax calculation tasks required for family child care businesses. In 2006 the IRS adopted our proposal to allow providers who hire part-time employees to file one annual form to report Social Security and Medicare taxes, rather than having to file quarterly reports. (For more information, see www.redleafinstitute.org.)

Join Us

Redleaf National Institute offers most of its services at no cost each year to thousands of family child care providers, tax preparers, trainers, associations, and support organizations. Our fees do not cover all of our expenses, and you can support our work by joining the Institute. Members receive discounts on Redleaf Press publications, news updates, a toll-free number to call for help, and much more. For more information, see page 162.

Membership Is Key

Membership in the Redleaf National Institute helps support our education and advocacy work that benefits family child care providers and allows them to be a part of a professional organization. Enjoy significant benefits when you become a member:

- 20% discount on all Redleaf Press books, software, and online courses
- Toll-free access to business experts who can answer legal, tax, and business questions
- *Business Bulletin* newsletter
- E-mail updates on breaking business news
- Customized IRS audit assistance
- Members-only savings on the Family Child Care Basic Business Essentials collection by Tom Copeland (see below)
- Membership kit

Now you have two membership choices:

• Annual Membership	109901-BR	$39
• Lifetime Membership	10990L-BR	$79

100% Tax Deductible

Special Offer for Members Only!

Members of the Institute can take advantage of a one-time special 33% discount on the Family Child Care Basic Business Essentials by Tom Copeland. This collection of six business titles from Redleaf Press will help new providers get their business launched and will help experienced providers be even more successful. This collection is regularly sold for $75.70. New members can purchase the collection for $50.75, plus shipping and handling. Save 33%! As a business expense, your purchase is 100% tax deductible!

Family Child Care Basic Business Essentials includes the following:

1. *Family Child Care Legal and Insurance Guide: How to Reduce the Risks of Running Your Business*
2. *Family Child Care Record-Keeping Guide, 7th Edition*
3. *Family Child Care Mileage-Keeper: The Complete Mileage Log*
4. *Family Child Care Marketing Guide: How to Build Enrollment and Promote Your Business as a Child Care Professional*
5. *Family Child Care Contracts and Policies: How to Be Businesslike in a Caring Profession*
6. *Family Child Care Inventory-Keeper: The Complete Log for Depreciating and Insuring Your Property*

#801001-BR RNI Members only $50.75

The Online Calendar-Keeper™

Writing, erasing, folding, and filing...

Tired of keeping records the old-fashioned way? Now you can enjoy all the benefits of the most trusted record-keeping system available for family child care providers on your home computer!

Containing all of the time-saving record-keeping, business, and tax information you've come expect from the *Calendar-Keeper*, *C-K Kids* also features:

* Meal planning
* Business tips from Tom Copeland
* Tax charts directly correlating to IRS forms, making tax time easier
* Automatic free updates several times a year
* A secure site, encrypted communications, password protected
* Automatic data back up—all information is saved for 4+ years
* Reliable, prompt technical support
* Daily, weekly, and monthly reporting tools and activity planning
* Financial management tools
* Tools to capture child information (medical, emergency contacts, birthdays)
* A chart and certificate maker
* E-claiming available with participating food programs

C-K Kids also includes menus and recipes that meet USDA guidelines; activities for each month; emergency phone numbers; waiting list and emergency drill records; space each month for showing holidays, birthdays, etc.; and updates on new Redleaf Press products and services. Information is completely updateable and pages can be printed with the click of a button. The only computer requirements are Windows 95 or higher and an Internet connection.

Initial subscription is $69.95; annual renewals are $39.95.

To sign up for a free 30-day demo, please visit
www.redleafpress.org

Redleaf Press • 10 Yorkton Court, St. Paul, MN 55117 • 800-423-8309 • www.redleafpress.org

Other Resources from Redleaf Press

GETTING STARTED IN THE BUSINESS OF FAMILY CHILD CARE

Redleaf National Institute

Whether just in the planning stage or already getting started in the business of family child care, you need this booklet. It covers topics such as promoting your business, managing your money, and planning for retirement. A great handout for support organizations. Also available in Spanish.

#108031-BR (ENGLISH, 25-PACK)	$28.95
#108001-BR (ENGLISH, SINGLE)	$2.95
#108033-BR (SPANISH, 25-PACK)	$39.00
#108032-BR (SPANISH, SINGLE)	$4.95

FAMILY CHILD CARE AUDIT MANUAL: STRATEGIES FOR PROTECTING YOUR BUSINESS IN AN IRS AUDIT

Tom Copeland, JD

This guide tells how to protect your business when faced with an IRS audit—what to do when audited, how the audit process works, and how to appeal—as well as how to avoid audits. A copy of the IRS *Child Care Providers Audit Techniques Guide* is included.

#105801-BR	$19.95

FAMILY CHILD CARE SHARING IN THE CARING: AGREEMENT PACKET FOR PARENTS AND PROVIDERS

The packet contains formal, two-part agreement forms to fill in contract terms for rates, holidays, vacations, payment dates, and illnesses to help you establish good business relationships to enhance your professional image.

#101401-BR (10 AGREEMENT-FORM PACKET)	$12.95
#101301-BR (5 AGREEMENT-FORM PACKET)	$8.95
#101201-BR (SAMPLE PACKET)	$5.95

THE REDLEAF CALENDAR-KEEPER 2007: THE RECORD-KEEPING SYSTEM FOR FAMILY CHILD CARE PROVIDERS

Redleaf Press

The *Calendar-Keeper* gives monthly expense charts for all purchases; monthly attendance and payment log for parent fees; Food Program tallies for meals, expenses, and claims; weekly/quarterly income record; important record-keeping advice; worksheets that make tax time a breeze; ready-to-use waiting list; recipes and menus with CACFP crediting; and so much more. Large format has space to record 38 children.

#100007-BR	$15.95

Product availability and pricing are subject to change without notice.

Other Resources from ❧ Redleaf Press

Do-It-Yourself Early Learning: Easy and Fun Activities and Toys from Everyday Home Center Materials

Jeff A. Johnson & Tasha A. Johnson

 Written by two experienced child care providers, this book explains the construction and use of a variety of engaging and kid-tested play props, equipment, and activities that help children become more confident, stretch their intellect, and encourage play and exploration.

#107401-BR   **$19.95**

Family Child Care Record-Keeping Guide, 7th Edition

Tom Copeland, JD

 This valuable resource includes information on more than 1,000 allowable deductions, a detailed explanation of CACFP (Food Program) expenses and income, ways to calculate work hours, and other topics such as bartering and military housing allowances.

#108601-BR   **$14.95**

Family Child Care Marketing Guide: How to Build Enrollment and Promote Your Business as a Child Care Professional

Tom Copeland, JD

 Dozens of marketing tips, information on setting rates, and a discussion of how to work effectively with organizations will help maximize enrollment and income and promote a family child care business.

#107201-BR   **$13.95**

Family Child Care Legal and Insurance Guide: How to Reduce the Risks of Running Your Business

Tom Copeland, JD, & Mari Millard

 From researching and purchasing insurance to protecting against lawsuits, this indispensable guide details the ways to ensure the health and prosperity of a family child care business.

#108501-BR   **$14.95**

Product availability and pricing are subject to change without notice.

Other Resources from Redleaf Press

FROM BABYSITTER TO BUSINESS OWNER: GETTING THE MOST OUT OF YOUR HOME CHILD CARE BUSINESS

Patricia Dischler

 From Babysitter to Business Owner offers tried-and-true strategies for implementing established professional business practices in the home child care environment.

#109801-BR   **$17.95**

THE PARENT NEWSLETTER: A COMPLETE GUIDE FOR EARLY CHILDHOOD PROFESSIONALS

Sylvia Reichel

 Written by a trusted educator with years of experience, this practical how-to guide provides a pathway for creating and implementing a parent newsletter—from advice on writing effective articles to design and layout suggestions to scheduling and distribution.

#536501-BR   **$24.95**

CREATING CONNECTIONS: HOW TO LEAD FAMILY CHILD CARE SUPPORT GROUPS

Joan Laurion & Cherie Schmiedicke

 Creating Connections, practical and easy to use, presents step-by-step methods for organizing and conducting effective family child care support groups.

#110101-BR   **$22.95**

More Business Resources

FAMILY CHILD CARE MILEAGE-KEEPER

Includes space for recording mileage, repairs, tolls, parking, and more for one year.

#104101-BR   **$2.95**

FAMILY CHILD CARE BUSINESS RECEIPT BOOK

Carbonless duplicate sets, 50 sets per book, 3 books per pack, 150 sets total.

#106101-BR   **$11.95**

FAMILY CHILD CARE INVENTORY-KEEPER

Tom Copeland, JD

Track furniture, appliances, and other property used in your business. Includes a photograph storage envelope.

#107001-BR   **$10.95**

Product availability and pricing are subject to change without notice.

800-423-83 **ess.org**